LONGMAN BACKGROUND BOOKS

Longman Background Books is a series of informative and factual books about aspects of Britain's past and present. In many countries students who are learning a foreign language are required to learn also something of the cultural activities, the attitudes of mind and the ways of life of the people whose language they are learning. This series is therefore an attempt to help the foreign student by describing and examining certain aspects of British life and history.

Other titles in the series are *An Outline of English Literature* and *Britain Today*.

All the books in the series are written within a general vocabulary of 2000 words (taken from *A General Service List of English Words*), to which the authors have added a limited number of words outside this list where they are connected with the subject and facilitate expression.

LONGMAN BACKGROUND BOOKS

An Outline History of England

A. G. Eyre, M.A.

 Longman

Longman Group Ltd
London
*Associated companies, branches
and representatives throughout the world*

© Longman Group Ltd 1971

First published 1971
New impressions *1973; *1974;
*1976 *(twice)*; *1977; *1978;
*1979

ISBN 0 582 53224 8

Printed in Hong Kong by
The Hong Kong Printing Press (1977) Ltd

Contents

Introduction

This book describes the development of the English people, their forms of government and their language. It shows how they became united with their neighbours in Wales, Scotland and Ireland, and how together they formed the British Empire and helped to form the United States of America. As the author explains on page 87, it is a history of *England* because England is the base on which the rest was built.

The book is written within the 2000 word vocabulary of the General Service List, but extra words are needed to cover its special subject. These are explained as they appear; the most important ones also appear in the index at the end of the book. This index contains a choice of interesting subjects and famous names which will be useful for future reference.

The books mentioned on pages 21, 112, 117, 128, 140 and 143 are all included among Longman graded supplementary readers. Students will find that they give a colourful background to the history of their times.

The study of the past helps us to understand the present. It is hoped that this book will help the reader to understand better the British people of today.

The writer is grateful for the help he has received from G. M. Trevelyan's *English Social History* and *Shortened History of England*, and also from Keith Feiling's *History of England*.

Acknowledgements

We would like to thank the following for permission to reproduce the illustrations:
Aerofilms Limited for page 8 bottom; Biblioteca Nacional, Madrid for page 14 bottom; Bibliotheque Nationale, Paris for page 44 bottom; Bodleian Library, Oxford for page 108 top; British Leyland for page 165; The Trustees of the British Museum for pages 22 top, 23, 38, 39, 48 bottom, 56 top, 64 top, 70 top, 74 bottom, 80 bottom, 92 bottom, 96 top, 97, 147; Cambridge University Library for page 49; J. Allan Cash for page 56 bottom; "Country Life" for page 81; The Courtauld Institute for page 80 top; Fox Photos for page 164 bottom; pages 57 and 64 bottom, reproduced by gracious permission of Her Majesty the Queen; Her Majesty's Stationery Office for page 152 top; The Illustrated London News and Sketch Limited for pages 138 top, 139, 153; Lambeth Palace Library for page 30 bottom; The Listener for page 159; John Little Associates for page 164 top; The Mansell Collection for facing page 1, and pages 44 top, 45, 48 top, 86, 102 bottom, 103, 108 bottom, 116 bottom, 124, 130, 131, 146, 152 bottom; The Marquess of Salisbury for page 74 top; The Ministry of Public Building and Works for facing page 1 top; The National Monuments Record and B. T. Batsford Limited for page 9; The National Portrait Gallery for pages 65, 70 bottom, 71, 96 bottom, 117; Pembroke College, Cambridge for page 14 top; Phaidon Limited for page 8 top; Photographie Giraudon, Paris for page 30 top; The Radio Times Hulton Picture Library for pages 92 top, 116 top, 158; Reece Winstone for page 138 bottom; The Science Museum for page 75; The Victoria and Albert Museum for pages 87, 93, 109, 125; The Warburg Institute for page 15; The Yorkshire Museum for page 1.

KINGS AND QUEENS OF ENGLAND 1066-1966

(By chapters, with the date when each began to rule.)

Note

The husbands of ruling queens like Victoria and Elizabeth II are not kings, they are princes. Any king's or ruling queen's sons, or their sons' sons, are princes.

The British Isles in 1600

Stonehenge

Bede, the writer of the 'History of the English Church'

I

A Roman gravestone

The Origins of a Nation

The great round temple of Stonehenge stands high in the hills of southern England, where the ancient Britons built it 3,500 years ago. Their remains can be seen in many places, but we have no written record of these early days until Julius Caesar visited the island in 55 B.C. By then many different tribes, especially the Celts, had crossed from Europe in search of empty lands for settlement.

For a few centuries the Roman armies stopped the westward flow of Europe's population. They brought Christianity to England, and their development of the country helped this religion to spread. Many of their army bases are now important cities: Gloucester and Worcester, Chester and Winchester and others. All these names are formed from the Roman word *castra*, which means an armed camp. Roman roads like the Fosse Way and Watling Street still mark the map, for no better ones were made until the eighteenth century. The greatest of these roads led mostly to London. Here the Romans chose a place on the north bank of the Thames where ships could lie in safety, and they built a walled trading city which would one day become the commercial centre of the world. But it was not the seat of government, though later ages developed a royal capital outside its walls.

The Romans came to govern and to trade, but not to settle. They were too few to change the language and customs of the people as they did in France and Spain. When they went they left behind a leaderless and defenceless people, and these were no match for the fierce northern tribes that now poured into the island. The Christian Celts, in spite of brave leaders like King Arthur, were wholly defeated. Those who escaped the sword were pushed back into the mountains of Wales and Scotland and across to Ireland, where their separate languages—Welsh, Gaelic and Erse—may still be heard.

The northern settlers were the people who formed the English nation. They were farmers and fishermen, soldiers and sailors; so they combined all the qualities that were necessary to develop and defend an independent island. At first they lacked unity; but when they were united in 1066 under the firm government of a Norman king, they became strong enough to resist all further attacks from Europe.

The Angles and Saxons from northern Germany spoke a language which we now call Old English. They took possession of all the land as far as the mountains in the north and west, and divided it into a handful of small kingdoms. Essex and Sussex, the kingdoms of the east and south Saxons, are still the names of English counties. Then they settled down to work their farms. But their separate kingdoms could make no organized resistance to the next wave of northern fighters, the Vikings. Some of these came from Norway and attacked the rocky coasts of Scotland and northern England; but the main body came from Denmark, sailed up the rivers of the east and south, and seized one little Saxon kingdom after another. At the last moment the Saxons were saved by the courage of King Alfred of Wessex, who defeated the Danes and forced their army to accept the Christian faith. Then he allowed them to settle in eastern and central England.

Both the Saxons and the Danes had been accustomed to worship northern gods like Woden and Thor, whose names have given us Wednesday and Thursday. They believed that courage, loyalty and rough honesty are the greatest virtues. How did the Saxons become Christian? Certainly they learnt nothing from the Celts, who refused to share their faith with such uncivilized people.

The question is answered by Bede, whose *History of the English Church* was written in Latin (the Roman language) while these events were still within living memory. Bede was a Saxon but he used Latin because this was the international language of the Church. Pope Gregory, he says, was attracted by some fair-haired young slaves on sale in Rome. The Pope, who was head of the Roman Church, heard that these slaves came from England, and he decided to send a party of his priests to help the English people. They made their base at Canterbury, and within a hundred years all England was united under one well-organized Church. Each district had its church leader, the bishop, and its central church building, the cathedral. The head of them all was the archbishop at Canterbury.

The centres of religious learning were the abbeys, where young men were trained to be priests. The land was divided into small districts called parishes, and each local Saxon chief built a parish church for his people and appointed a priest to serve them. The Saxon parish is still the smallest unit of local government, as well as of the church organization; in some villages the Saxon church with its round tower is still in use, and at its door, or the door of any church, one may see a list of those who have the right to vote.

The priests took their orders only from the bishops, who were treated as royal officials and sat in court beside the chiefs. But Alfred did not want to depend on the Church for all his officials. He opened a school for the sons of chiefs, to teach them the arts of orderly government. He also brought learned monks from abroad to work in the abbey libraries. These monks were not ordinary priests, because they did not preach; they lived quietly in their abbeys and studied holy writings. King Alfred had a great respect for education. He himself wrote some school books in Old English, including a translation of Bede's *History;* and he began the *Anglo-Saxon Chronicle* in which the history of the land was recorded by monks for the next three hundred years.

Under Alfred and his sons, the Danes and Saxons settled side by side in peace. The land was then mostly thick forest, full of wild animals which men could hunt for food. Gradually this forest was cleared, and villages appeared in the open spaces and beside the rivers that carried trade to the towns; but nothing remains of the great wooden halls in which a Saxon chief would live with his men. Walled market towns were built in all the old Roman centres. Their townsmen were proud freemen who served no local chief; they traded inside the walls, farmed outside them, and took up arms to defend them when necessary. Under Danish influence, Alfred built a navy of fighting ships to protect his shores; he also provided horses to move his soldiers quickly, though they had not yet learnt to fight on horseback.

Under the weak King Ethelred there was trouble once more. Fresh waves of fierce Danish fighters attacked the south. Instead of fighting them, Ethelred collected a tax and paid them to go away, but each year they wanted more. The poor were ruined by this tax and even the rich suffered. No wonder that, when he died, the council invited the Danish leader Canute to become their King.

Canute went on collecting the tax in order to pay for foreign wars that soon made him King of Denmark and Norway too; but he worked hard to unite his Danish and Saxon peoples. He trusted their great lords, who ruled the various former kingdoms in his name, and with their help he tightened the loose control that Alfred's sons had gained over the whole country. He became a Christian and used the Church to draw all men together. He kept Winchester as his capital, where English and Danish were the joint languages of his court. One of his relatives was married to King Duncan of Scotland, who was later killed by Macbeth. Another was married to Godwin, the great Lord of Wessex, whose son Harold became the last Saxon king. Canute did much to improve trade with Europe, where English wool and cloth were already in great demand. He also married Ethelred's widow, daughter of the Duke of Normandy.

A duke is the highest rank of noble below a king, and the Norman dukes owed loyalty to the kings of France; but in fact they were completely independent. The Norman ruling class were Vikings who had settled down and adopted the French language and religion. They had also learnt the French way of fighting on horseback, though their followers still fought on foot. Normandy was the most highly organized state in Europe, and the life of all classes was controlled by strict rules. There were a number of powerful lords, but the most important class were the knights. These knights were small landowners who were also experienced professional soldiers, for they held their lands on condition that they fought for their lords whenever necessary. Their lords owed the same duty to the duke. Their country was small and they still had the Viking taste for adventure. A day's sail could carry them to England. It was a temptation.

4

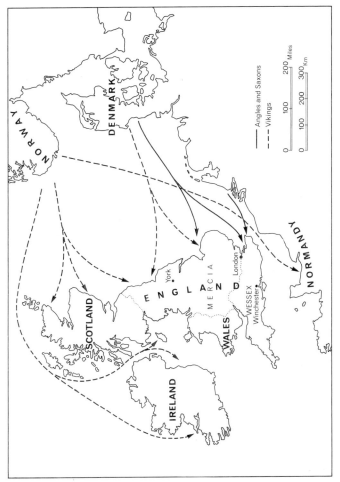

Origins of the Early Settlers

Canute died and left two sons; but they were evil men, and soon Ethelred's son Edward was called from Normandy to be King. He had been brought up in an abbey and was more like a monk than a king, so that people called him Edward the Confessor. He was formally married to Godwin's daughter, but he made no attempt to give her a child. He spoke Norman French. His tastes and his friends were Norman. He gave Sussex lands to Norman abbeys and put a Norman in command of the Sussex harbours. He even appointed a Norman archbishop.

The council, which included both Saxon and Danish lords and bishops, were getting seriously worried. When it was reported that Edward had promised to leave the kingdom to his Norman cousin, they decided to take action. They forced Edward to dismiss his archbishop and appoint a Saxon instead; but they were too disunited to prevent the spread of Norman influence and power.

At Christmas 1065 they were gathered for the opening of the King's new abbey at Westminster, two miles outside the walls of London. Here Edward had already built himself a royal home. But he was too ill to attend the opening of his abbey, and a few days later he died. On his death-bed he chose Harold of Wessex, his wife's brother, to be King in his place. The council approved of this choice, and Harold was crowned next day. Like Canute, he did not belong to the royal family of England; but he was a Saxon lord, and he was chosen by Edward and the council. By English custom he was lawfully crowned.

The council knew well that others would claim the crown. Duke William of Normandy would claim it because of Edward's secret promise; the Kings of Denmark and Norway would claim it because of their family ties with Canute. If Harold had had the full support of his lords, he could probably have saved his kingdom; but many were jealous of his position and some clearly favoured his foreign rivals. When the attack came it found England disunited. As Shakespeare writes:

> 'This England never did, nor never shall,
> Lie at the proud foot of a conqueror,
> But when it first did help to wound itself.'

When Norway's King landed and seized York, Harold rushed

north and destroyed him and his army. Three days later Duke William landed on the Sussex coast, and Harold rushed south again. Without waiting to collect support from doubtful lords, he met the Norman army near Hastings. His tired men fought bravely but they had no experience of fighting against cavalry, and the Norman cavalry were the finest fighting horsemen in Europe. When night came King Harold and the best of his men lay dead on the hill-top. And on Christmas Day 1066 William the Norman was crowned in Westminster Abbey.

*Part of the Bayeux tapestry showing the
inside of a Norman Castle*

Castle Rising in Norfolk

2

The Normans

A Norman doorway into a church in Yorkshire

As soon as William had been crowned, he began to organize the government of England on the system that had been so successful in Normandy. This is called the feudal system, and it was based on the ownership of land. William took the land away from its English owners and divided it among his Norman lords, including his bishops and abbey leaders.

The lords' land was then divided among the 5,000 knights who had fought at Hastings. Each knight had to swear loyalty to his lord; he also had to give him forty days of army service every year. The lords themselves had to swear loyalty to the King and they had to supply knights for his service. A knight's land was called his manor, and the common people belonged to the knight on whose manor they lived. They had to serve him as farm-workers but not as soldiers; only the King himself could call them out to fight in times of trouble. There was also a small class of freemen, who did not have to work on the knight's farm.

Most of the King's own land was forest, which he kept for hunting. The forest laws were very severe. Nobody was allowed to cut down a tree, and anyone who killed the King's deer was punished by the loss of an eye or a hand. These laws were hated by everybody, but if William had not made them there would be no forests or wild deer in England today. The popular New Forest, south of the old capital of Winchester, has been *new* ever since William took it for himself.

In Normandy, William had had much trouble with lords who grew too powerful. He was determined not to have the same trouble in England. Instead of giving each of them one large piece of land, he gave them several small pieces in different parts of the country. The only exceptions were the great lords of Hereford, Shrewsbury, Chester and Durham who had to guard the Welsh and Scottish borders.

All the lords had the right to attend the King's council, and it was his duty to ask their advice. William held council meetings nearly every day wherever he happened to be. Usually only a few lords were present besides his secretaries and state officials. But three times a year he held a ceremonial council for Christian feasts and wore his crown: in Winchester for Easter, in London for Whitsun, and in Gloucester for Christmas. Then every lord had to attend.

Winchester castle was still the seat of government. Here William set up his government office, which controlled the collection of taxes and kept account of all expenses. From this office, men were sent out in 1086 to make a detailed record of all the wealth of England. Their work, the *Domesday Book,* gives us a complete description of the country. It records all land and property, every mill and cottage, every cow and pig. It also records the rights and duties of every landowner and every court.

Such records were grouped by counties and by manors, as these were the usual groups for tax collection. The King fixed an amount for each county; his sheriff divided this amount between the manors; and the owner of each manor collected the money from his people.

The sheriff was the King's representative in each county and he held the rank of a lord. He ruled over the county courts without interference from the Church, for William had given the bishops their own courts. This was an important step, for it allowed the English Common law to develop freely while the church courts were tied to the laws of Rome. But it also led to serious trouble because any servant of the Church could claim the right to be tried by his bishop and not by a public court.

County courts took important cases but manor courts dealt with local affairs, and even the lords had their own courts to protect their feudal interests. When William was crowned, he swore to respect the ancient laws of England. But his Norman sheriffs and landowners did not know these laws, so a group of local people had to attend each court as advisers.

The *Anglo-Saxon Chronicle* of those days gives thanks for 'the good peace that he made in the land', but William's troubles did not end at Hastings. The northern lords, who had not fought there, rose against him twice. His revenge was prompt and terrible. After his army had passed, no human being was left alive and no house was left standing between York and Durham. Norman castles were built all over the country, especially on the Welsh border, and the citizens of London were disturbed to see William's famous Tower rise beside their walls.

But castles were not his only means of controlling his new kingdom. The Church was a stronger and more effective weapon. England was already Christian, and the people were accustomed to obey their priests. It was easy to appoint Norman bishops in place of the Saxons, and the parish priests would do what they were told. William appointed an experienced lawyer called Lanfranc as Archbishop of Canterbury, and he treated him as the head of his government. When William was away in Normandy, Lanfranc ruled for him. Meanwhile the bishops quickly made their influence felt through their new courts and their seats in council, where they held the rank of lord.

Abbeys were especially encouraged, and Battle Abbey near Hastings stands as William's own memorial to his victory. His brother Odo, Bishop of Bayeux in Normandy, arranged an even more famous memorial. His Bayeux Tapestry is history written with wool upon cloth. It shows us the events of the Norman conquest in two hundred feet of bold and colourful pictures.

During the next hundred years new abbeys were built all over England. Mostly they were in the country, as the monks had to grow their own food and live quiet, religious lives. One of their main duties was to make copies of the Bible and other holy books. This was slow work, for they wrote carefully with feather pens and used coloured inks to make it beautiful. They also educated boys to become monks or parish priests or clerks. There were no ordinary schools, so the abbeys supplied clerks for the royal offices and the courts, and for landowners and merchants too. These clerks were regarded as church servants although they had no religious duties.

An abbey church was for the monks' own use, and they did not preach to the people; that was a parish priest's work. They spent their lives in their libraries and on their farms. They never met the general public, but their kitchens fed the very poor and their hospitals cared for the sick. Even the rich lords respected them and often gave money to help their work.

When William died he left Normandy to his eldest son, Robert, and England to his second son, William Rufus. Rufus was an ugly and evil character, who scorned religion and took delight in cruelty. But he built Westminster Hall, which was the national seat of justice until the nineteenth century.

No one was sorry when Rufus was shot dead while hunting in the New Forest, and his brother Henry took his place. Henry's first thought was to reunite England and Normandy. Most of his lords owned land in both countries and they gladly supported his plan. In 1106, just forty years after Hastings, an English army under Henry's command defeated Robert and seized Normandy.

Henry had already done much to earn the loyalty of his English people. He was born in England and knew the English language and law. He married the daughter of King Malcolm of Scotland and Queen Margaret, who beloged to the Saxon royal house. His father had given a charter of freedom to London; he now gave charters to towns that helped him to conquer Normandy, and he let London elect its own sheriff. These charters were official papers which gave freedom from various feudal duties and allowed the towns to run their own affairs. They helped to increase trade, both at home and abroad, and coal from Newcastle began to reach France in exchange for wine, though wool and cloth were still the basis of the country's trade.

Henry made Normans and English equal before the law. His travelling officials checked the work of the sheriffs and their courts, so that gradually the same law was applied all through the land. He was well liked because he kept the peace, but he must bear part of the blame for the terrible years that followed his death.

Henry was the last of the true Norman kings, for his only son was drowned at sea. He planned to leave the kingdom to his daughter Matilda, whose husband ruled all the land between Normandy and the River Loire. But England was not yet ready to be ruled by a woman, and on Henry's death the lords appointed his nephew

Stephen as their King. Stephen was popular and he had an English wife, but he was weak. Matilda soon bribed half the lords to support her, and for nineteen years the two sides fought each other. Men and cattle were killed in thousands; towns and villages were destroyed; harvests rotted in the fields.

At last Matilda's husband died, and the lords who had refused to accept Matilda were willing to accept her son. The archbishop arranged a settlement, and the lords agreed to pull down all the castles—about a thousand—that they had built during the war. Stephen then conveniently died. 'A mild man,' said the *Saxon Chronicle*, 'soft and good, but he did no justice.' The *Chronicle* itself, that had begun with the great deeds of King Alfred, now ended with the sad story of human misery under Stephen.

Surprisingly, there was one side of English life that had not suffered but had even made progress. The great abbeys of Tintern and Fountains, whose ruins still point their proud arches to the sky, are only two of the hundreds that were built in these troubled times. The lords cared little for human life, but they hoped to save their own souls by building abbeys for the glory of God.

In spite of Stephen, the Normans had left to England a framework of government which a strong king could develop with success; and a strong king was coming. They had also set England firmly on the path of European civilisation, which would have been long delayed if they had been content to forget Normandy and settle quietly in their island. When Henry's English army defeated Robert, it was setting a pattern for the future. For five hundred years after the conquest, English kings struggled to hold and extend their French lands by battle and by marriage.

A twelfth-century meal

Crusaders attacking a castle

3

The Rule of Law

Richard I

Few kings of England have done such lasting work as Henry II. He found the country in a state of ruin and confusion. He left it with a system of government and a habit of obedience that were able to keep the peace long after his death.

Henry had a strong will and a fierce temper; but he was well educated, especially in the study of the law. He was also the most powerful ruler in Europe. He received all north-west France from his father and all south-west France from his wife. He ruled, in fact, all the land between Scotland and Spain. No lord could dare to disobey such power, and Henry soon brought order to his English kingdom. The French King in Paris claimed that Henry owed him loyalty for his French lands, but Henry took no notice of such claims.

The upper classes in England still spoke French, which united all parts of Henry's empire. Free travel encouraged trade and the exchange of ideas. French visitors to England said that they found a good-tempered people, who were fond of outdoor sports and games and jokes. The English in return were greatly influenced by the music and literature of France.

Arts, skilled trades, commerce and agriculture all now made rapid progress as the land-owning classes became more settled. A knight's feudal service of forty days was of little use to Henry, who needed regular soldiers to guard his French possessions. He encouraged his lords to pay a special tax instead of sending him their knights. This allowed him to hire professional soldiers while the

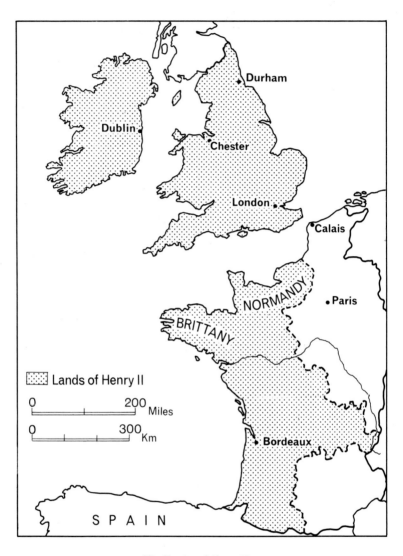

Durham

Dublin

Chester

London

Calais

NORMANDY

Paris

BRITTANY

Lands of Henry II

0   200 Miles

0   300 Km

Bordeaux

S P A I N

The Empire of Henry II

knights remained at home and improved their manors. It suited the King and it suited the knights, who were already settling down to become country gentlemen.

Let us look for a moment at the pattern of country life a hundred years after the conquest. The stone castles of Stephen's time had been pulled down and replaced by stone manor-houses, in which the long hall and other buildings opened on a walled courtyard. The house and yard were often surrounded by a wide ditch, full of water, and the only way in was across a bridge to the courtyard gate. The knight and his family lived in the hall together with his household staff. Sometimes he had his private room at one end of it, but usually only a curtain separated his sleeping-place from the rest.

Some knights, of course, still chose to go to war whenever they could. Some were content with the fashionable sport of the tournament. This was a sort of friendly battle-practice, where knights in full armour charged each other on horseback and tried to knock each other to the ground. Their faces were hidden by their armoured head-pieces, so each knight had a special sign painted on his shield, by which he could be recognised. This was useful in battle too, of course, and the tournament was good practice in the arts of war; but it was chiefly a social occasion. Ladies came in their best clothes to watch. The field was gay with flags, and each knight had his own brightly coloured tent, where he could put on his armour.

Most knights, however, were content to do their public duty in the county and to develop their manor. Only the Welsh and Scottish borders needed castles full of armed men for their protection, and even here Henry's iron will made itself felt. The King of Scotland and the chiefs of Wales were forced to swear loyalty to him; and at Christmas in the year 1171 the chiefs of Ireland gathered to kneel before him in Dublin.

In one way the English upper classes were developing differently from their fellows in Europe. To keep the feudal framework unbroken, a man had to leave all his land to his eldest son. The younger sons had to make their own way in the world. The quiet ones joined the Church or made a modest fortune in commerce; the bold ones looked for adventure abroad as soldiers or, in later ages, as explorers. Improvements in agriculture brought to these upper classes new wealth with which to raise their standard of living. Their demand for better clothing and household goods encouraged skilled workers in the towns, who formed the basis of a new middle class.

But life was not so easy for the serf, the common man who belonged to the owner of the manor where he lived. The customs that ruled his life were much the same as they had been in Saxon days, but they were more strictly applied. He could not marry his children without his master's permission. When he died, his best beast was taken by his master. He had to grind his corn at his master's mill. He had to work on his master's land without pay for a fixed number of days each year.

In return for this he had his rights. He held strips of plough-land in the common fields. He had his share of the village grass-land for his cows, of the waste-land for his pigs and chickens, of the woodland for his logs. His master had a duty to protect him, and he could find a remedy for his complaints in the manor court. He was not free, but he was safe. He could not leave the village, but he could not be forced to leave it either.

The serf's home was built of split logs, for the art of brick-making had been forgotten since the Romans left. There was no chimney, and the smoke found its way out through the grass roof. In west and north England the houses were scattered, but in the south and east they were grouped close around the manor-house and the church.

In districts of open grass-land the landowners kept sheep in thousands, for English wool was the best in Europe. Belgian and Italian weavers depended on it for their finest cloth. Even the serfs made a good profit from their sheep, and the women spent their days spinning wool and weaving cloth for sale, as well as for their own use.

All this was part of the feudal way of life. It had developed gradually through the years, but too often they had been years of violence and uncertainty. Under Henry, for the first time, conditions became settled enough for a steady increase in trade and in population. But he is best remembered for his reform of the courts and their law. Reform is a word that appears frequently in English history. To reform a thing is to change it for the better, and we shall see in this book how through the ages the English struggled to reform their Church, their feudal society, their industrial conditions and, of course, their government.

Henry sent out his own judges to make regular tours of the country, and any freeman could take a case to them if he did not trust the local courts. Serious offences and land cases could only be dealt with by judges, so lords could no longer use their own courts to steal land from their weaker neighbours. The serfs did not profit by these reforms, but they would profit in future ages when all were free.

Most important of all was Henry's jury system. The jury was a group of people who helped a judge in court. Nowadays they listen to witnesses and then decide whether the accused is guilty, but this practice did not develop till the fifteenth century. In Henry's day the members of the jury were witnesses themselves, and no man could be tried unless a jury of twelve men swore that there was a true case against him. This was real progress, for men had often been tried with no witnesses at all. In criminal cases the trial itself was still made with a hot iron in front of a priest; if the man was burnt by holding the iron, he was guilty. This cruel practice went on until 1215, when the Pope forbade all priests to take part in it. But Henry did stop *trial by battle* in private cases, as this let any tough fighter treat his neighbours as he pleased.

In England now there are two kinds of law: the laws made by the government, which are called Acts, and the Common Law. This Common Law was first gathered together by Henry II. It reflects the changing customs of the land which have been expressed in court judgments through the ages. Henry believed so strongly in the rule of law that he kept no army in England, but he laid down the exact weapons and armour that every free man should hold ready for the defence of his country.

Only two things spoiled his own peace: his quarrels with his sons and his quarrel with Archbishop Becket. It was natural that his sons should sometimes stir his temper, but the matter of Becket was more serious. Many practices of the church courts were an insult to Henry's rule of law, for they often let even murderers go unpunished. Henry decided that criminal clerks must in future be tried by his own courts. Public opinion supported him, and most bishops agreed. So did the Pope, who was then living in France to escape the German Emperor. But Thomas Becket was a proud and fierce-tempered man like Henry himself; he refused to agree and fled abroad. Five years later he returned and preached against the King in Canterbury Cathedral.

When Henry heard of this he lost his temper completely: would no one get rid of this troublesome priest? Four knights who heard his words went straight to Canterbury and killed Becket inside his own cathedral. Henry was sincerely sorry and he let the monks of Canterbury beat him publicly for his wicked temper. But Becket's murder forced him to drop the matter of church courts, which remained a serious cause of annoyance to the common people.

Becket was really a rough fellow, but after his murder he was regarded as a holy man. Bottles of Canterbury water were soon sold for high prices, and men claimed that prayers to Becket had healed their sickness. Two hundred years later the poet Chaucer described in his *Canterbury Tales* how men still travelled there from all England to pray at Becket's grave.

By the end of the twelfth century all the royal offices had been moved from Winchester to Westminster, which thus became the nation's capital. In modern times we call London the capital, because this name covers not only the old city of London but all its extensions, including Westminster. At that time, however, Westminster was quite separate.

The strength of Henry's work was soon proved by his sons. Richard I was only in England for ten months of his ten years' rule, but the government carried on without serious trouble while he was away on the crusades. These crusades were religious wars, in which the Christian kings of Europe tried to win control of the holy city of Jerusalem from the Turks. Earlier English kings had not joined them, but Richard was a popular and able soldier who loved adventure. His success in battle won him undying glory but it annoyed the jealous King of Austria, who seized him on his way home and imprisoned him in a castle.

During his absence the government was in the hands of Archbishop Walter, who was well supported by the knights and by the middle-class townsmen. He gave charters of freedom to towns that helped to pay for Richard's crusade. He also let London elect an independent head of its city council and gave him the title of Mayor. When Richard was imprisoned, his brother John tried to seize power, but the lords and London's mayor remained loyal. They helped Walter to defeat him and to buy Richard's freedom. It was a sad day for England when Richard was later killed in France. He had won the love and respect of all classes, as Sir Walter Scott has so excitingly described in *Ivanhoe*.

Clothes fashionable at the time of King John

A Chief Justice at the time of Edward I

4

The Birth of Parliament

Simon de Montfort

For the next seventy years England suffered from weak kings who were unfit to rule, yet the troubles of Stephen's time were not repeated. Henry had taught his people the rule of law. He had set them an example of good government. In future, if any king failed to follow this example, his people were ready to remind him of it.

How should they remind him? Surely this was the council's duty? And if he refused to listen, then clearly the council should be made stronger. But a strong council needs popular support, and the people had always regarded the King as their protector against the lords. There was only one answer to this problem: representatives of the people would have to join the council. Then they could resist any king's misrule without being dependent on their lords.

This widened council was called parliament, which was a Norman French word for a talking-place. Weak kings let its powers increase, and strong kings kept these powers within reasonable bounds. Between the two its influence developed by gradual degrees, until kings at last realized that a strong parliament was their own best defence against their enemies. King and parliament together were then at last able to control the troublesome lords and the Church, whose wealth and power hindered the nation's progress. The story of the people's struggle is a long one, and it begins with Richard's brother, John.

King John had been his father's favourite son. He grew up to be cruel and selfish, and thoroughly unpopular. When he murdered his sixteen-year-old nephew, Prince Arthur of Brittany, the King of France seized all his northern French possessions. Only the extreme south-west with its great port of Bordeaux remained loyal; not for love of John, but for the value of its wine trade with England. A port is more than a harbour; it is a harbour-town where merchants can store their goods and do their business. Without Bordeaux the trade of John's last French lands would have been ruined.

Then the archbishop died, and John invited the Pope to choose between two men who both seemed suitable for the post. But the Pope chose a third man, Stephen Langton, without even asking John's opinion. This was against custom. John refused to accept Langton, and the people supported his view. Most of the bishops fled abroad rather than take sides in such a quarrel. Other priests steered a middle course; for five years no church bell rang in all the land, but they continued to hold services outside the locked church doors. At last the Pope persuaded the King of France to attack England. John yielded to this threat, for he had no army ready. He accepted Langton and promised to pay Rome a large yearly tax.

Two years later, for the first time in English history, the people took the side of the lords against their King. John was determined to revenge himself on France, and for this purpose he had been demanding more feudal taxes and army service than custom allowed. He had made about seventy towns buy charters of freedom at immense cost. Now an army of angry lords marched to London, which welcomed them with open gates. Any earlier king would have called out the common people to fight for him, but no one would fight for John except his hired foreign soldiers.

Henry II had taught his lords to respect the law. They now taught John that a king too must respect the law and rule by it, not by his own fancy. At Runnymede, on the Thames near Windsor, the lords forced John on 17th June 1215 to sign the Magna Carta, the great charter of English freedom.

The charter covered a wide field of law and feudal rights, but the two most important matters were these: no tax should be made without the approval of the council, and no freeman should be arrested or imprisoned except by the law of the land. The serfs had not yet become freemen, but the matter of tax touched all men, whether free or not.

24

The charter was strictly practical. It contained no grand ideas about the rights of man, but its spirit has kept it alive until today. A king was brought to order by orderly means, and what happened once could happen again. Four centuries later the Stuart kings dared to set themselves above the law, and the name of the charter was on the lips of those who sent King Charles to his death. In the name of the charter the American colonies declared their independence, and in 1965 a memorial to J. F. Kennedy, the American President, was placed beside the Thames at Runnymede.

John signed unwillingly and no one trusted him; so the charter itself gave the lords the right to use force against him if he broke his word. They did not have to wait for long. The Pope, whose friendship John had bought, declared that the charter was unlawful and advised John to tear it up. Archbishop Langton disagreed with the Pope and begged John to listen to reason, but he begged in vain.

Fighting broke out again, and at first John's forces were successful. But the lords asked for help from France and the King's fortunes began to turn. Then, suddenly, he died.

His son Henry III was only nine years old, but all parties promised him their loyalty. Under the wise influence of Langton the charter was accepted, John's foreign army was dismissed, and all was peaceful until Henry became old enough to rule.

Then all the old troubles began again. Henry, like his father, hoped that with Rome's help he could defeat the lords and their charter. Year after year he poured English gold into the Pope's treasury and let him fill church posts with hated foreigners. He filled his own household with foreign advisers. He made expensive and useless attempts to win back the French lands that his father lost. After thirty years of misrule his treasury was empty, and England was ready for another Runnymede.

This time the scene was Oxford, and the aim was more carefully planned. The men of Runnymede had been concerned with the law and men's rights; those at Oxford were more concerned with political control. Under the leadership of Simon de Montfort, the King's brother-in-law, they forced him to dismiss his foreign advisers and to accept their own council of advisers instead.

De Montfort's new council took control of the Treasury and all state officials, including the Chief Justice and his staff, and the county sheriffs. Then they settled down to work out their reforms. The towns supported de Montfort, so did the students and teachers of Oxford and Cambridge, and young people everywhere. His enemies took up arms against him, but in 1264 he defeated the royal army at Lewes and took the King prisoner.

He now called the parliament that made him famous. Besides the usual lords and churchmen, it included knights from each county and representatives from each borough, which is the special name for a chartered town. The word *parliament* had been used before to describe the King's council, and such representatives had occasionally attended it to discuss their particular business. But they had never before been called, officially and all together, to discuss the general government of the kingdom; nor had any parliament met without the King.

The English have always liked committees, where they can solve problems by discussion rather than by violent action; their social and political life in modern times is run entirely by committees. Parliament developed through the centuries as an expression of this national feeling. De Montfort did not invent it, but he was one of the first who helped it to take shape. A year after Lewes a group of rival lords, with the King's elder son Prince Edward, defeated and killed de Montfort at Evesham. But his work was not in vain. The next King showed that he had learnt de Montfort's lesson: to respect the law and to consider the advice of his people.

Edward I was the opposite of his father. He was a soldier by nature, with a towering figure and an iron will. He required strict discipline in the land under his command and he judged all men by their efficiency. He did not intend to yield any of his powers to parliament, but he hoped to rule more efficiently by keeping in touch with popular opinion. He liked to discuss taxes with the knights and borough representatives, and he depended on them to explain his royal purposes to their people. In the days before newspapers, when travel was dangerous and difficult, their regular visits to the capital helped to develop a sense of national unity. The political education of the country had begun.

Edward's reforms touched everyone. He dismissed dishonest officials, both in his household and in the state service. He made new land laws which lasted for six centuries. He forbade anyone to give land to the Church without his permission, for the Church was becoming too rich and powerful. He cut down the powers of its courts, and in his own courts he appointed judges who were not churchmen. He would not allow interference by the Pope, as his weak father and grandfather had done. He distinguished between crimes and simple offences, and made every village responsible for its own peace.

The old feudal tax system was gradually replaced by a tax on property. Customs-duty was collected on goods going in and out of the country, which are called imports and exports. The main export was wool; the imports were wine and cloth. The King encouraged foreign traders but he disliked the Jewish money-lenders. The Jews had been unpopular since the crusades for religious reasons; Edward now drove them out of the country, and they were only let in again by Cromwell 350 years later. By then the control of banks was firmly in English hands, so that England has never had a Jewish problem.

Although he was a soldier, Edward made no serious attempt to win back the lost French lands. He aimed instead to bring Wales and Scotland under his rule. As we shall see in a later chapter, he conquered Wales without much difficulty; but Scotland resisted more strongly, and Edward died while still fighting for control of the highlands.

His son Edward II was a weak and lazy king who left the work of government to household favourites. Soon a party of lords, like de Montfort's party, was formed against him. Parliament approved of their plans, which demanded the public appointment of all the King's household as well as of the state officials. He was soon in trouble in other ways too. His father-in-law, the King of France, attacked the lands around Bordeaux. The Scots rose in arms and the lords refused to fight them, so that Edward's army was cut to pieces at Bannockburn. At last even the Queen turned against him. For some time she had been living with her lover, Roger Mortimer. Now she and Mortimer seized Edward with the help of foreign soldiers, and parliament forced him to hand over the crown to his son. A few months later he was murdered in Berkeley Castle.

Edward III was only fifteen, and for three years his mother and

Mortimer ruled in his name. Then Edward arrested them. He imprisoned his mother for life, and sent Mortimer to London to be hanged in public like a thief.

The results of the Black Death

The capture of Calais

Sir John de Cobham, a fourteenth-century knight

5

The Hundred Years' War: Part I

Young Edward now claimed the French crown through his mother, for her brothers had all died without a son. He had good reasons to want control of France. The French were doing their best to spoil his country's wool trade. Their ships threatened the Channel, that narrow strip of water which separates the English shores from the mainland of Europe. They were always stirring up trouble in Scotland. They held the Pope as a prisoner and misused his influence on the English Church. They regularly broke their faith over English rights around Bordeaux.

Edward could not forget that all western France had belonged by right to Henry II. Weak kings had lost most of it in war, but a strong king could regain it in the same way. If he could not get it peacefully through his claim on the crown, he was ready to fight for it. The French now refused his claim, and in 1337 the Hundred Years' War began.

Parliament at first objected to the cost of the war but was soon influenced by its success. Edward began by marching into Belgium to free the wool trade, and by destroying enemy ships in the Channel. Then his armies swept across western France. In the Battle of Crécy he and his son the Black Prince (so called because of the colour of his armour) defeated an enemy force more than twice their number; but numbers meant little to Edward, whose kingdom's population was about three and a half million against the eighteen million of France.

Over fifteen hundred French knights lay dead at Crécy. Their charges never reached the English lines, for the English were using a new weapon in this war, the longbow. It could send an arrow through the best plate armour. Edward encouraged it as a village sport; he even made a law against football so that it should not interfere with the bowmen's practice.

Edward went on to take Calais, the nearest port to England, but then fate stopped the war. A terrible disease, which Englishmen called the Black Death, swept across Europe with more murderous effect than any army. A third of England's population died and for seven years there was peace. Then fighting began again. This time the Black Prince was taken by surprise when he found the Loire in flood, with all its bridges broken. But in a fierce battle near Poitiers he defeated the French, and took their King as a prisoner to London with many of their nobles. Once again the French army had been greater in numbers, but its feudal organization had been no match for the more freely organized English.

Edward's army was composed of companies of professional soldiers under experienced captains. He did not have to pay them much, for they depended on the riches that they could seize from conquered towns and wealthy nobles. Prisoners were the best prize of all; King John of France had to pay half a million pounds for his freedom, and all his noble followers had to buy their freedom too. He also had to promise to make no more trouble in Scotland, and to give up his claims to Calais and south-west France.

Edward in return gave up his claims to the French crown. But the agreement had hardly been signed when the Black Death struck once more and left England too weak to hold her conquests. Before Edward's fifty years of rule were over, the Black Prince and his best captains were dead; all France was lost again except Calais and Bordeaux and a few other ports.

While the King was busy with his wars, parliament developed rapidly towards its present form. The common people's representatives got into the habit of meeting privately to discuss their business before they joined the lords. By 1350 they also had a Speaker, whose duty was to speak for them all and to express their agreed opinions to the lords.

Within the next ten years the old parliament divided into three parts: a House of Commons, a House of Lords and a small permanent council. This third body was composed of the King's official advisers; it met regularly in the Star Chamber, which was a room ornamented with golden stars. The others only met when parliament was called.

The Commons began to consider their own bills, as well as those which the council prepared for them. When these bills were passed by both houses they became Acts of Parliament, with all the force of law. The King could make orders-in-council, but they had less permanent value than Acts. The Queen today still makes orders-in-council; in time of trouble she can give special powers to the government by a stroke of the pen, when parliament would take weeks to produce the same result. Today, too, when the Queen opens parliament, we can see it as it was in the early fourteenth century. Custom forbids the Queen to enter the House of Commons, but she takes her seat in the House of Lords, and there the Commons are called to listen to the royal address.

As long as parliament supported his wars, Edward was content to increase its powers. He gave it complete control of taxes. But it still depended on him to see that its wishes were carried out, for the state service and the courts and the armed forces of England have always owed their loyalty to the crown and not to parliament.

The Commons refused to discuss foreign affairs. They were happy to pay the cost of the King's wars so long as the country profited by them; but war was his personal responsibility and not theirs. Their aims were order and justice and the growth of trade. They needed Calais and Bordeaux to protect this trade, but they were not greatly worried by the loss of French lands.

In local government, too, Edward left his mark. The kind of men who filled the Commons had been used for some time as unpaid servants of the crown, to keep public order everywhere. Edward now appointed them Justices of the Peace and gave them the local powers of his sheriffs and judges. The English people's great respect for the law is the result of the honest justice that these J.P.s have given them through the centuries.

The Black Death had a sudden and violent effect on society. It struck all classes, and three archbishops died within a year; but the poor suffered most. In some places whole villages disappeared.

Landowners everywhere were short of workers. Those serfs who escaped the disease now shared between them the lands of those who died; some even employed other serfs to work for them. They objected to feudal service on their master's farm. Many landowners avoided trouble by renting their farms to a new middle class of farmer, the yeoman. These yeomen were freemen who had improved their social position by hard work, like the skilled men in the towns. They might employ serfs and they might even have their sons taught to read by the parish priest, but they were not ashamed to work with their hands on the land.

Some landowners stopped growing corn and used all their land for sheep. Others let the serfs pay a small rent instead of their feudal service. Then they hired men instead; but the rent was not enough to cover the wages that such men demanded. The Church, however, still tried to keep its feudal rights and refused to accept rent instead of service; the monks had grown too fat and lazy to work themselves as they did in former times.

Parliament passed an Act to control wages and food prices, but the serfs formed unions and went on strike against fixed wages, and against the whole idea of feudal service. Their spirit spread to the towns, where workmen were demanding higher wages from merchants and manufacturers. Gradually the land was becoming organised on a commercial instead of a feudal basis. The long struggle between employee and employer had begun. For £15 a serf could buy his freedom from the crown, and with high wages and good wool profits this was possible for a hard-working man. But new ideas of human rights were spreading from the university of Oxford and men were asking why they should have to buy their freedom.

On Edward's death the country was soon in serious trouble. French ships attacked the southern ports. Richard II was only ten years old, and the government was in the hands of his uncle the Duke of Lancaster, commonly known as John of Gaunt. To fight the French, a tax was collected from every male over fifteen years old. In 1381 this tax was one shilling a head, and the people refused to pay.

Crowds gathered in the countryside. They broke into abbeys and manors to burn the feudal records. The men of Kent marched to

London under the leadership of an old soldier named Wat Tyler. There they were joined by crowds from other counties. They were not all hungry and poor, but they objected to taxes without freedom. They demanded an end of feudal service, but they were willing to pay rent for their farms instead. Many were old soldiers who had learnt self-respect in the army. The workers of London opened their gates in welcome.

Richard's council were taken by surprise and did nothing. John of Gaunt had travelled north to keep out of the way; he had royal ambitions for his own son and would not have been sorry to see Richard destroyed. Meanwhile the crowds grew angry, and the wilder men among them became violent. They killed the archbishop and the treasurer, they broke open the prisons, and they attacked every lawyer and foreigner they could find.

Somehow or other the council had to get rid of them. It was decided that Richard should promise to accept their demands if they went home quietly; but the council had no intention of keeping this promise. A public meeting was held, and in the middle of it the mayor of London killed Wat Tyler. For a moment it looked as if the serfs would kill all the King's party. Only Richard's personal courage saved the situation. 'Sirs, will you shoot your King?' he cried as he got on his horse. 'I will be your captain.' The simple countrymen followed their fair-haired boy King out into the fields, and the danger was over.

Parliament declared that the whole trouble was caused by evil official practices and it recommended a general pardon. Only the leaders were tried and hanged. The King's promises were not kept, but the landowners had learnt a lesson; gradually they gave up their claims to feudal service and accepted rent instead. Serfs were still not free, but many of them found their freedom by escaping to some distant county where an employer would ask no questions.

In 1389, Richard declared himself to be of age, and for eight years he ruled as a moderate king. Then he married the daughter of Charles VI of France. From this time he seemed to adopt French tastes and ideas, and to use his power to get rid of anyone who might be a danger to him. A number of powerful lords were arrested. These included John of Gaunt, who died in prison. John of Gaunt's son, Henry of Lancaster, was sent out of the country. But in 1399 he returned, and was joined by most of the lords. Richard was put in the Tower and forced to resign his crown. Henry of Lancaster now became King Henry IV, and Richard died mysteriously a few months later.

London in Chaucer's time

Spinning wool

6

Chaucer's England

A few months after Richard's death, a poet was buried in Westminster Abbey. He was Geoffrey Chaucer, the 'father of English literature', whose critical and amusing verse has given us a clear view of fourteenth-century life. Chaucer was a London wine-merchant's son who married a relative of John of Gaunt. He travelled widely in Europe on royal service and became controller of customs-duty in the port of London. He was also a knight of the county of Kent, and his son became Speaker of the House of Commons.

In 1386 he travelled to Canterbury to pray at the cathedral where Thomas Becket had been murdered, and his best-known lines are in the introduction to his *Canterbury Tales*. Here he describes the twenty-eight people who gathered one April evening at an inn near London Bridge to travel with him.

He was a religious man or he would not have made this journey, but he had no respect for officials of the Church. He describes them as rich, lazy, dishonest and immoral. Only the parish priest earned Chaucer's praise as a kind and hard-working Christian, but he was poor like his brother the ploughman. The party also included a knight and his son, a lawyer, a doctor, a farmer, a sailor, a merchant, a weaver, a miller and an Oxford student. All are described in detail: their look and manner, their dress and speech, their character and behaviour. Chaucer is curious. He observes, and he records his observation without fear or favour. He has no political or moral purpose; he has only a sincere desire to let others share his experience and enjoyment of life.

Geoffrey Chaucer belonged to a new middle class of society that was developing in England while kings and nobles fought their wars, and while serfs were struggling for their liberty. It was a class of educated men who were not church servants, for the Church no longer owned all the schools. Some were professional men, such as lawyers or state officials; far more were concerned in trade, both at home and abroad. The protection of foreign trade was Edward III's strongest reason for war with France. His gold coins remind us of this, for they show him standing in armour on a ship. He had no navy, but he hired merchant ships to guard the Channel.

Since Saxon days English wool had been sent abroad, especially to Belgium, to make fine cloth. Much of this cloth had then come back to England for sale. Edward now stopped this import so as to encourage the manufacture of good cloth in England. Merchants brought Belgian weavers to teach their skills to English workers. The cottage weavers were jealous, but they could not match the high quality of the merchants' new product, which soon became a valuable export. As the King collected customs-duty on this trade, it was in his interest to increase it. Woollen cloth became the chief industry of the land until the nineteenth century, when cotton took the place of wool. Norwich, the centre of the best sheep-farming country, was the largest city after London.

In big towns, the weaving and every other trade were controlled by guilds. A guild was a society of men who practised the same trade. They controlled the standards of products, especially cloth; they also controlled prices and wages, and the training of workers. They gave board and lodging to young workers, and made rules for sick pay and against night work. Their leaders formed the borough council, whose chairman was the mayor. In London he was given the special rank of Lord Mayor.

The London guilds still exist and have always been influential. Their fifteenth-century Guildhall is the seat of the city council. They choose the Lord Mayor and his sheriffs every year and they play a valuable part in the city's life. Most of them are ancient, but the Guild of Scientific Instrument Makers shows that their ancient system keeps up to date.

London was already spreading outside its city walls. A stone bridge had been built across the Thames in 1176, and the city controlled land on both sides of the river, where its ships could lie. Inside the walls, its citizens were completely free from royal interference.

Two miles outside, the river led to Westminster with its government offices. Here parliament met and the royal judges held court. But the King had no property in the city, so between Westminster and the Tower he travelled by water. The city gladly lent money to pay for wars that protected trade; but they kept four bags of wool (called woolsacks) beside Edward III's seat in parliament, to remind him of their reasons for lending it. The chairman of the House of Lords, whose title is the Lord Chancellor, has sat on a woolsack instead of a chair ever since.

Leather goods and coal were exported as well as wool and cloth. Foreign traders and bankers were welcomed in London, especially those from Venice and Florence and from North Germany, though their presence was often misunderstood by workers who feared foreign competition. They helped to organise the international trade shows that were held every year in the big market towns.

Coal from Newcastle came to London by ship and was used to heat the houses, so that new rules for fire prevention and safe building were needed. The citizens had strict duties in such matters, and the Mayor could call on them to carry out public works as well as to defend the walls. Every large town had a Watch Committee, which employed watchmen to guard the streets at night. Even now, those who live beside Canterbury cathedral may hear the old cry, 'Twelve o'clock, a fine night, and all's well', as the watchman passes by their windows.

The lack of police made it easy for serfs to escape their masters. It also allowed robber bands to disturb the countryside. Travel was dangerous, but the lord in his castle did not worry. He was busy making comfortable new rooms inside, and his walls were strong enough to resist attack until Cromwell's heavy guns were used against them in the seventeenth century. Even the manor-house was safe against most attacks. Its outer windows were only wide enough to shoot through, though large windows faced the courtyard. The owner's private rooms might have glass windows. He no longer shared the hall with his men, and his rooms were pleasantly furnished, for he had learnt much from the civilized habits of French nobles.

Chaucer's fashionable characters wore a short coat, with tight stockings up to the waist, instead of the long loose clothing of their fathers. Rich materials like silk and fur were popular, and gay colours. One stocking leg might be red, the other blue. Gardens of bright flowers showed their interest in nature, and this was reflected in the poetry of Chaucer and his fellows, who described their joy in woods and rivers and the song of birds.

In the month of May, says Chaucer, a poet puts away his books

'And seeth the fressche floures, how they springe.'

This is Middle English, which had replaced the Old English of King Alfred but had not yet settled its spelling, for it had rarely been written down. A line of Chaucer may look difficult, but when it is spoken it is easily understood. Any modern reader can sympathise with the poet when he goes out 'and sees the fresh flowers, how they spring'. His work became popular at once and his *Canterbury Tales* was one of the first books to be printed by Caxton a century later.

Alfred's English had already been mixed with Danish when the Normans came. For the next three hundred years the language of the upper classes was Norman French, and educated men wrote only in that or Latin. English was not written, and so it was able to develop freely without interference by schoolmasters, who would have tried to fix its forms. Gradually it lost most of those word endings—which languages like German and Italian still use—for male and female forms, and for the different persons of the verb.

Most Normans learnt some English, but they were too proud to speak it openly until the wars of Edward III made French unpopular. Then the King ordered that only English should be spoken in the courts and schools and other public places, and the nobles began to use it among themselves. So the difference between Normans and English disappeared; from this time, all were Englishmen. Books in English became fashionable, including William Langland's verses about *Piers the Ploughman*. This work described the evils of life in every class of society, but with its deep moral purpose it lacked the freshness of Chaucer.

Chaucer's travels and experience had given him a wide knowledge of the language, which now contained many Norman French words to express new ideas, especially in law, politics and religion. There were differences between the various kinds of English spoken in the north, south, east and west, as there are now; but the language of the centre would be understood in every part. Chaucer and Wycliffe spoke the English of Oxford, Cambridge and London, which became the standard of the educated classes. In the following centuries it gradually developed, especially in the hands of the translators and printers of the Bible, from Middle English into Modern English.

The Battle of Agincourt, 1415

Joan of Arc

7

The Hundred Years' War: Part II and the Wars of the Roses

A Tudor Rose

When Henry of Lancaster claimed the crown in 1399, he began a royal family quarrel that disturbed the country for almost a century. Jealous cousins would not accept his claim, and many lords took their side. Fighting broke out again and again between the King's enemies and his supporters. France, Scotland, Ireland and Wales seized the opportunity to cause more trouble. No wonder that, when Henry IV died, his son Henry V declared war on France. It was the only way to take the lords' minds off their quarrels and to unite them once more in a national effort. The French, he said, had broken their promises, so honour demanded that he should claim the French crown.

Henry was a born soldier and a popular leader. At Agincourt in 1415 he defeated a French army five times greater than his own. Although guns had recently been invented, the battle of Agincourt was won by the longbowmen against heavily-armed French knights. The French had not learnt the lesson of Crécy, and their dead lay in thousands beside a mere hundred English. The bells of London were set ringing, and Henry attended a service at St Paul's Cathedral to give thanks for his victory.

After this success he tried to reach agreement with Paris, but in vain. His armies then began to seize all northern France. His guns and mines broke open castle gates and city walls. He was not merely a soldier but a great organizer, who kept his men well clothed and fed. No king has been more faithfully described by

Shakespeare than Henry V, who walked round his camp at night to encourage his men and to see that the guards were properly at their posts.

By 1420 France had had enough. A peace agreement arranged that the French King should keep his crown for life, that Henry should marry his daughter and become King of France on his death, and that meanwhile Henry should rule for him. Henry's reputation for discipline and justice soon won the respect of the French people, but two years later he died. The French King died soon after.

Henry's baby son now became Henry VI of England and France. It was most unfortunate that the new King was only nine months old, for a strong ruler was needed to keep the peace on both sides of the Channel and to develop an orderly union of the two countries. Henry's ablest uncle governed in Paris, and here Henry was crowned when he was ten years old. But in England things went from bad to worse. Every great lord kept a private army with which to fight his neighbours, and parliament objected to the cost of holding France.

In France, an eighteen-year-old girl called Joan of Arc gathered an army around her and attempted to drive out the English. She was captured and sold to the English, who handed her over to the Church. The Church accused her of having a devil in her. She was found guilty and burnt to death. But her courage was an example to her people. After Henry's uncle died in Paris, they gradually won back their lands; by 1453 only the port of Calais remained under English rule. The Hundred Years' War was over.

The King had grown up weak in mind and body, and he was now quite mad. His cousins began a fresh fight for power. The rival parties were the houses of Lancaster and York, which were both descended from Edward III. The flag of Lancaster showed a red rose, and the flag of York showed a white one, so the struggle between them became known as the Wars of the Roses. This struggle went on for thirty years. Open battles were few, but murder and revenge were common. Political trials after each disturbance took many noblemen to their death.

In 1461 the Calais army commander, Lord Warwick, decided to interfere. After fierce fighting, the King's forces were defeated and his cousin Edward of York was crowned with Warwick's support. Edward IV was nineteen years old, very tall, good-looking and a fine soldier. He also had an eye for pretty women and he refused Warwick's plans for a political marriage with the French royal house. Warwick then changed sides and tried to bring back poor mad Henry, who was a prisoner in the Tower. Edward killed Warwick in battle, and a few days later Henry died mysteriously.

In 1483 Edward died and his twelve-year-old son became Edward V. But before he could be crowned, he and his brother were shut up in the Tower by their uncle, who had himself crowned instead as Richard III. A month later the two boys were murdered. There is no proof that Richard was responsible for this double murder; but he had already been blamed for other deaths in the royal family and it was easy to blame him again. His enemies now looked around for a leader. They found one in Henry Tudor, a powerful Welsh lord whose mother came from John of Gaunt's family. He had been living in France to escape the quarrels of his relatives. Now moderate men of all parties offered him their support, if he would marry a sister of the murdered boys and thus unite the Houses of Lancaster and York.

He accepted this offer and landed in Wales, where his supporters joined him. Then he defeated and killed Richard at the battle of Bosworth. So Henry the Welshman became Henry VII, and England settled down to a new age of orderly government under the royal House of Tudor.

Sir Thomas More and his family

*Scholars at Magdalen School, Oxford
at the beginning of the sixteenth century*

8

An early printing press

Education and Social Freedom

Up to the end of the fifteenth century, England's trade and other affairs were tied to Europe, where her kings fought to hold lands that they had won by marriage or by war. At home, the Church and the lords ruled over a population of serfs. There was little peace or freedom except in London and the boroughs.

By Shakespeare's time all this had changed. The feudal powers of the Church and the lords had been destroyed, though the House of Lords still formed part of parliament. The common man was free. England was looking beyond Europe for new fields of trade and settlement. The whole pattern of her society had been gradually changed during the eighty years before Shakespeare's birth in 1564. It was a peaceful change, and it was carried out by the crown with the support of the Commons and of the new middle classes. But it would not have been possible without the educational development of the fifteenth century.

The Church had become increasingly unpopular since it supported a French Pope during the French wars. As a result, many rich men gave their money to build schools instead of giving it to the Church. New grammar schools were opened in all big towns. Often they were built by guilds or by private merchants, who were proud of their towns and wanted to give local boys a chance. They gave free education to the 'poor'; but everyone was considered poor who could not afford a private teacher for his children. So the grammar schools were filled with the sons of traders, yeomen farmers and skilled workers, who gradually formed a valuable new force in society—well-informed public opinion.

In 1382 William of Wykeham followed the example of King Alfred and opened a public school in Winchester. (The name *public school* is misleading. Nowadays, most schools are controlled by the State and are free; public schools, however, are not state-controlled and their pupils must pay.) William was a bishop, but he was also the King's chief minister. He realised the importance of training those who were likely to fill important positions when they grew up. So his school was planned for 'the sons of noble and powerful persons' as well as for clever boys from ordinary homes, who did not have to pay. He also opened New College at Oxford, and encouraged his Winchester boys to go on there.

King Henry VI saw the value of Wykeham's work. In 1440 he opened his own school at Eton, near Windsor Castle, and his own King's College at Cambridge.

In both Universities the students had at first lived in public inns, where their lives were ruled by wine, women and song more than by study. Gradually the college system produced order and discipline, which resulted in high standards of learning. The secret of the success of Oxford and Cambridge lies in this system. The university council includes college representatives and it controls the teaching, but the colleges control the learning. They provide board and lodging and they make sure that each student studies for his examinations; his work is guided personally by one of the college staff. But they also offer him active social life and help him to develop all his interests in art and sport.

If these new schools and colleges had only taught Latin, like the old church schools, their value would have been limited; but since they were free from church control, they welcomed the new learning of the Renaissance that was now sweeping across Europe. *Renaissance* is a French word that means rebirth. The arts and sciences of ancient Greece were being born again after long ages of neglect, and the country of this rebirth was Italy. In 1453 the Turks seized Istanbul, which had been the centre of Mediterranean civilisation for a thousand years. Many of its Greek teachers fled with their libraries to Italian universities, where they were warmly welcomed, for their language and literature were almost unknown.

Englishmen who studied in Italy brought the new learning back with them to Oxford and Cambridge, and from there it spread to schools all over the land.

Thomas More's *Utopia*, written in 1516, gives us some idea of its influence. Utopia was his name for an ideal land, where there would be freedom of religion and a national system of education for both boys and girls. The book was immensely popular, and translations of it were sold all over Europe. More was a rich man and he encouraged artists like Holbein, who became official painter to Henry VIII. He also encouraged Thomas Linacre, who studied medicine in Italy, became Henry VIII's personal doctor, and opened the first doctors' training college in London.

But his best friends were the Dutchman Erasmus, who taught at Cambridge, and John Colet, who taught at Oxford and was later in charge of St Paul's Cathedral. These two men were leaders of a movement for reform of the Church. They studied old Greek copies of the Bible, which showed how badly the teaching of Christ was understood by the Church. They preached against the wealth and laziness of the abbeys, against the sale of church posts and the worship of old bones. They felt strongly that the Church should set an example of Christian virtue; it should also express its faith in simple ways that human reason could accept without difficulty.

There was a great demand for books so that the new learning could be passed on to all the new schools. In the past, the only supply of books had come from the abbeys, where they were copied by hand. But this was slow work, and the monks could only copy what the Church allowed. Then in 1476 William Caxton set up the first English printing-press in Westminster. He had learnt the art of printing in Germany, and in the next few years he produced about eighty different books. Many of them were his own translations of foreign works, but perhaps the most popular were Chaucer's *Canterbury Tales* and Malory's *Morte d'Arthur*, which describes the adventures of King Arthur and his Knights of the Round Table.

Caxton was not only a printer, he was also a serious student of the English language. There were no dictionaries to guide him, but he set a standard of spelling and grammar for others to follow. He wisely avoided religious argument and printed nothing that could cause trouble. The first printed translations of the Bible were made in Germany and Switzerland by the reformers Tyndale and Coverdale; they could not be printed in London until 1539, when Henry VIII had broken free from Rome. Then, by the King's order, a translation was placed in every church so that it could be read even 'by the boy that drives the plough', as Tyndale had planned.

From that day to this, the Bible has been the best-seller of all books. In many homes it was the only book until modern times, and the beautiful English of those early translators has had a powerful influence on other literature.

While this educational development was going on, England was fortunate to have two strong and sensible kings, who took a keen interest in science and the arts, and who also thoroughly understood their people. Henry VII quickly realized that his people were tired of quarrelsome lords, with their bands of armed men; the middle classes wanted nothing but peace and orderly government.

So many lords had been killed in the Wars of the Roses, or had lost their lands to the crown, that with the Commons' support Henry was able to destroy their power for ever. Their feudal rights and duties came to an end. They no longer had to supply soldiers for the King, or pay a tax instead, as this had been one cause of all the trouble. Now they were forbidden by law to keep any armed followers. The royal court of the Star Chamber was given power to deal severely with any rich man who wronged his poorer neighbours.

The troubles of the past century had not been caused by a lack of law but by its misuse. Every great lord had kept a private lawyer to prepare false claims against his neighbours' lands, and had used armed men to frighten the courts which heard these claims. Henry took care not to employ any such lords in important positions; he used only his own well-educated and trusted officials. The feudal basis of society was broken completely, and the state took over the landowners' responsibilities.

The noble families did not disappear but they mixed more freely with the commercial and professional classes. Their younger sons became merchants and lawyers, and married the townsmen's daughters. Every rich townsman aimed to improve his social rank by settling in a country manor-house. Thus the wealth of the towns found its way back to the country and helped to keep a healthy balance between trade and agriculture.

The wool merchants were developing a new system of trade. With their capital they controlled the flow of wool from the sheep-farmer to the weaver, and the flow of cloth from the weaver to the foreign market. Only their capital and their experience could provide the connection between producer, manufacturer and buyer which was essential to the growth of commerce.

In Henry's new national state there was no need for an army, for he ruled with popular approval. He made no claims to land in Europe, for he realized that peace was essential to good trade. Instead of fighting, he married his children to the royal families of Scotland and of Spain, which was already becoming a powerful rival. To encourage the weaving industry, he increased the customs-duty on imported cloth; he reduced the rights of foreign traders in London; and he encouraged ship-building by forbidding the carriage of imports in foreign ships. Most of all, he encouraged adventurous merchants to explore new lands. In spite of the Pope, who had divided the unknown world between Spain and Portugal, he sent Cabot to explore the coasts of Canada and of Newfoundland, which later became England's first colony.

Except in the first few years of his rule, he made little use of parliament and ruled through his council instead. This was only possible because he was a good businessman. He made enough money from his crown lands, from customs-duty and from court punishments to pay the costs of government, so he hardly ever had to ask parliament for extra taxes. Sometimes he forced the rich to lend him money, but he always paid it back.

He also increased the powers of the Justices of the Peace. They were made responsible not only for public order but for matters that concerned trade: the control of guilds and of workers' affairs, and the care of roads and bridges. Their courts gave honest justice, and the poor could bring cases without payment. Printed law-books helped to train lawyers at the Inns of Court. These old inns had been turned into colleges for law students in Edward III's time, and they kept the same discipline as a university college.

Henry VII gave England peace and orderly government. He encouraged education and exploration. He increased trade. But he did not find time to deal with the greatest problem of all, the

Church. In Italy and France the Renaissance was a rebirth of art and science, but in Germany and England it was a rebirth of religion too. Since Henry VII and his parliament had reformed the feudal habits of the noble families, his son was able to work through parliament to reform the Church.

Friars building a church

Wells Cathedral in Somerset

9

Wine cup for use in church

The Problem of the Church

In the seventh century the church leaders in England had freely decided to follow the religious leadership of Rome, which united the Church in the whole of Europe. This was natural, for Rome had brought Christianity to the island. But in the sixteenth century, England cut her ties with Rome; the Church of England became a national body under the control of parliament and the King. What caused this change?

Through the ages, the Church in Europe gathered wealth and power that attracted the jealousy of kings. The rulers of England, safe in their island, used the Church for their own political purposes. Most of them resisted the Pope's interference in their national affairs, but they did nothing to weaken his rule in Rome. The German emperors and French kings, however, fought endlessly for the control of Rome; whoever held it in his power could control the influence of the Church in every land.

If the popes had been left in peace, they might have provided the religious lead that England wanted. But in their struggle for independence they needed money and allowed the Church to follow any practice from which money could be gained. In spite of their efforts they were not strong enough—except in the thirteenth century—to resist the armed forces of the other two great powers. As a result, their treatment of English interests was influenced by the political pressure of England's enemies and rivals.

By the sixteenth century the new national spirit of the English people had become impatient of such conditions. The greed and laziness of the Church was hindering their social and political progress at home while the Pope, under foreign influence, hindered their commercial progress abroad. Thus when Henry VIII decided to break free from Rome he was supported not only by parliament and the people but by many honest leaders of the Church itself.

The Church was already rich and powerful when the Normans came. It was rich because it taught men to fear death; to save their souls they gave it land and money. It was powerful because it had the only schools and provided the only educated men. Its bishops sat with the lords in court and council, and its clerks kept all official records and accounts. The machinery of government depended on men whose loyalty was divided between Church and State.

It was not wholly a bad system, and William the Conqueror adopted it for good reasons. He had to fill official posts for which there was little money; he had also to fill church posts that were well provided with money and property. What could be easier than to make an archbishop his chief minister, or to appoint some treasury clerk as priest of a rich parish? In this way some of the Church's wealth was put to the service of the State. Church duties might be neglected, but the system saved the need for extra taxes.

William also arranged to make the bishops swear personal loyalty to him. He gave them all the feudal powers of lords. They had seats in his council, as some of them have in the House of Lords today. They held extensive land. They even had to provide knights for the King's service. The archbishop had to provide sixty knights, but this was easy as Canterbury was rich. It was so rich, in fact, that on Lanfranc's death William Rufus refused to appoint anyone in his place, and for four years he filled his royal pocket with cathedral gold.

The Normans were strong kings and they resisted any outside interference in their church affairs; yet their relations with Rome were smooth enough for an Englishman to be appointed Pope in 1154 as Adrian IV. But the thirteenth century found two weak kings in England just when Rome produced her strongest leaders. For the first time the true loyalties of the people were put to the test.

We have already seen how King John was forced to promise a large yearly payment to the Pope, who in return supported him in his efforts to resist the lords who had made him sign the Magna Carta. But the archbishop believed that his country needed the charter, and he had the courage to stand up for his beliefs. The angry Pope declared it to be unlawful but he could not frighten the people as he had frightened the King. The charter was not a religious matter and therefore, in English eyes, it was not his business.

The next Pope, however, did know his business: he aimed to reform the Church all over Europe. He realized that in England the bishops were too busy with state affairs; that most village priests were too badly educated to understand the Bible; and that the monks in their abbeys were out of touch with the people. As a remedy for these troubles he sent a large number of travelling preachers, called friars. These friars were followers of two holy men, St Francis and St Dominic. Their rules did not allow them to possess money or property. They walked bare-footed from town to town, preaching and teaching. They explained the Bible in simple language. They cared for the poor and the sick. All England welcomed them.

This was the sort of religious leadership that was wanted, but other events quite spoiled the effect of the friars' good work. Public opinion against Rome became more and more angry as the weak Henry III let church posts be filled with uneducated Italians, who never carried out their duties. But the next King had a strong character. When Rome ordered its churchmen not to pay his taxes, Edward I took prompt action. He declared them 'outlaw', which meant that any man could take their lives or property, for they were outside the law. In 1305 the King of France took even more serious action; he seized Rome, closed its church offices, and set up a new Pope at Avignon in France. For the next 110 years the Church in England was thus under the influence of its people's enemies. It continued to send money secretly to Avignon, even when the two countries were at war, but by then it had already lost the respect of parliament and the people. Wat Tyler's men were expressing the disgust of the poor when they cut off the archbishop's head and burnt the abbeys' records. The disgust of the educated classes was shown, less violently but more lastingly, by Geoffrey Chaucer.

There were many reasons for this feeling. Bishops and abbey leaders sold church posts, or left them empty and filled their pockets with the unused salaries. Men paid for their sins with money instead of tears and prayer. Chaucer's *pardoner* is only a mild example of a dishonest churchman; others were more actively wicked and immoral. The pardoner had official permission to sell God's pardon for men's sins. In his bag he had bits of cloth which were said to have belonged to the mother of Christ,

'And in a glass he hadde pigges' bones'

which he sold as the bones of famous holy men. The public courts could not touch such men, and the church courts merely encouraged them.

The abbeys, except in the north, no longer cared for the people as they used to do. In Norman days they had been known for holy learning and for helping the poor. In Chaucer's time the rich abbeys were harder masters than other landowners, and they kept dozens of servants to look after the fat and lazy monks. The towns on abbey lands hated them most. Other towns could win charters of freedom from the King. Why could not they too be free?

The new educated middle classes in the towns were jealous of the Church's hold on the state service. The Church, they said, should stick to its religious duties; the State should take over the abbeys' wealth and use it to pay professional state servants. The House of Commons said so too, but it had to wait more than a century for a strong king to act.

Men also disliked the use of Latin, which few village priests could really understand though Chaucer regarded them as honest men. English had recently been made the language of the courts. Surely it could be the language of the Church as well? No man might possesss even a Latin Bible without his bishop's permission; and when John Wycliffe translated it into English, the bishops burnt every copy that they could find. Wycliffe was the head of a college at Oxford, and he preached there that a man should read his own Bible and be guided by his conscience. No priest, he said, should stand between God and man. He was a hundred years too early to have his Bible printed, but his followers carried their handwritten copies wherever they preached. Only John of Gaunt's protection saved him from the bishops' anger.

It is so easy to point to the faults of the feudal Church that men often forget what they owe to it today. Let us consider two things, its education and its buildings. Until Chaucer's time its cathedrals, abbeys and parish churches provided the only schools. Some of these, like Westminster, were given new life by Henry VIII's reformation of the Church, and they are among England's finest schools today.

Clever boys, if they were lucky, could go on to Oxford or Cambridge to continue their studies. Here the teaching was given by monks and friars. We have seen how the friars came to England in the thirteenth century. They came as preachers, but the best of them were soon invited to teach at Oxford, for they were better educated than any monk. Four colleges were opened to house the students who gathered to hear such learned men. The friars held broader views than the monks, but even the friars could not go outside the narrow field of study that the Church allowed. The arts and sciences of the Renaissance might find their way into fifteenth-century town schools, but most church schools considered them too dangerous.

Eleven Oxford colleges and ten at Cambridge were built before the year 1500. The money for them came mostly from kings and noble families, but they owe their beauty to the Church's experience of building. The tourist who travels around modern England sees everywhere the fine cathedrals and churches which stand as memorials to that experience. By the same date, thirty-four cathedrals had been completed. Many of these were built on William the Conqueror's orders. For the cathedral at Canterbury, not only the builders but even the stone had come from Normandy. Without its wealth, the Church could not have produced such masterpieces.

The parish churches have a different history. More than ten thousand of them date from before the days of Henry VIII. Some were built by bishops or abbey leaders, others by local landowners; often they stand beside the manor-house and its farm as the central building of an English village. Like the cathedrals they grew with the centuries, but Saxon stonework and Norman windows still tell their story. There were a hundred churches in London when John was King, but most were lost in the great fire of 1666.

As the centuries passed, the Church learnt by experience and developed new ideas of building. But its religious and social ideas did not make such progress. So long as Rome's mind was governed by fear of other powers, the Church in England would follow its ancient feudal ways. A break was bound to come.

We may wonder that it did not come sooner; but the time was not ripe until the new learning of the Renaissance had done its work. Only a king with strong popular support could declare his Church's independence of Rome. Only a king like Henry VIII could then build a navy to guard that independence against the growing power of Spain, Rome's chief supporter.

Part of the English fleet at Dover

Henry VIII with some of his court

The Reformation of the Church

Cardinal Wolsey

When the eighteen-year-old Henry VIII became King he was extremely popular, for he had all the qualities that his people admired. Foreigners reported that he was the best-dressed King in Europe and that his chief interests were 'girls and hunting', but this was only half the truth. He distrusted foreigners, as most Englishmen did at that time; but he spoke three foreign languages. He was a first-class horseman and musician. He could discuss religion and ship-building with equal skill. He was a clever politician who trusted parliament and made full use of it. Most important of all, he thoroughly understood the hearts and minds of his people. He ruled through the House of Commons, without an army, and his people remained loyal to him through all the difficult years of the Reformation.

For the first twenty years of his rule, Henry was content to enjoy life and to leave all government business to his chief minister, Thomas Wolsey. Wolsey was the son of a small trader, but he was clever, and the most ambitious churchman in all England's history. In his fine houses at Hampton Court and Whitehall he lived more grandly than the King himself. He was not content to be chief minister and archbishop; his aim was to become Pope.

At first all went well. He kept a balance of power in Europe, so that no country should become strong enough to threaten his shores; and this has been England's official aim ever since. In 1513 both the French and their Scottish friends were heavily defeated in battle, but this left France too weak. Wolsey now gave his support to Charles V, the German Emperor, who was also Charles I of Spain, for he hoped that Charles would help him to become Pope. Too late he realized that the balance of power was broken and that Spain had become strong enough to destroy England. But Henry was wiser than his minister; he saw that England's safety must now depend on sea-power rather than on politics. His interest in ships and guns produced a navy that not only defeated Spain but influenced English history for centuries ahead.

During all these years, both Henry and Wolsey had kept a firm hold on church affairs. They supported the Pope, but they saw that reforms were needed. Wolsey warned all bishops and abbey leaders to improve their discipline. He stopped the appointment of any more unofficial churchmen—those clerks who had no religious duty, but who claimed freedom from the public courts. He closed thirty abbeys with the Pope's approval and used their wealth to build Christ Church College at Oxford.

Henry took no action against the Church, but he was ready to support those who did. When Parliament declared that criminal clerks must be tried in public courts, Wolsey wanted to refer the case to Rome. Henry refused. The kings of England, he said, had never had any master but God alone. He was a great friend of More and Colet, and he defended Colet against the attacks of angry bishops. His quarrel was with the Church's behaviour, not with its faith. He wrote a book against the German reformer, Martin Luther, and the Pope gave him the Latin title of *Fidei Defensor*, defender of the faith. This title may still be seen on every English coin.

When Henry became King he married Catherine, the daughter of the King of Spain and widow of his elder brother. The Pope had given special permission for him to marry his brother's widow, as this was against the laws of the Church. She gave Henry a daughter, Mary, but all her sons died at birth, and Henry badly needed a son to follow him. He began to feel that God had not approved of his marriage and that the Pope had been wrong to allow it.

There was only one possible remedy. The Pope must declare that the marriage had been allowed by mistake and was unlawful; Henry would then be free to marry again. Wolsey and his bishops supported this view. The Pope could easily have agreed, as he had done for two recent Kings of France in similar cases. But Emperor Charles V was Catherine's nephew, and his army had seized Rome. The Pope was in his power and did not dare to annoy him by helping Henry. Instead he asked Henry to visit him.

Henry was extremely angry. He dismissed Wolsey and made More his chief minister; then he called a new parliament. He still had no wish to break away from the Roman Church, which is now commonly called the *Catholic* Church. He wanted a reformed national Church within the catholic framework. For the next five years he did his best to persuade the Pope to accept his ideas; but the Pope remained under Charles's influence, and all Henry's efforts were in vain. He began to listen instead to the Cambridge reformers, Cranmer and Latimer, Ridley and Coverdale.

Henry's trouble over his marriage made him realize something that most English people had known for years: that foreign interference in English affairs had gone on too long and must be stopped for ever. The parliament of 1529 felt this most strongly. In seven years it destroyed the feudal power of the Church completely. The Church Council accepted Henry as its head. Archbishop Cranmer declared that his marriage to Catherine was unlawful and accepted his new wife, Ann Boleyn, as Queen. And at last, when all attempts at agreement failed, Parliament passed laws which cut its last ties with Rome.

Most of the bishops accepted these changes without difficulty. They had always been appointed by the King, and many had served as state officials. There was no change of faith; only a change of leadership.

It was different for the abbeys. They had always taken their orders direct from Rome. Now few of them served any useful purpose. They no longer supplied the only books or teachers, for the printing-press and the grammar school had taken their place. Most of them were too far from a town to provide religious services for the people. Yet they still had six hundred separate houses, and the yearly profit from their land was worth two million pounds in modern money. Some monks were holy men and some were wicked, but most were just comfortably lazy and useless. Half their houses were now closed by order of parliament; the rest closed one by one.

The old monks were given enough to live on in retirement. The best of the young ones became parish priests. Female education suffered the most serious loss, for religious women ran the only girls' schools, and these were now closed. The best boys' schools were kept open by the King, and abbey money was set aside to pay for them. Some modern public schools, like the King's School at Canterbury, were ancient abbey schools before Henry gave them new life and a new title.

Two-thirds of the abbey lands were sold, the rest was kept by the crown. An immense amount came into the possession of the middle classes. New teachers replaced the old monks at the universities, and new colleges were built for the rapidly increasing number of students. Most of these came to be trained for the public service, which was no longer under church control. Church services went on as usual, except that they were in English instead of Latin. Those who wanted to change any part of the faith were called Protestants, but they had little influence yet. The King and parliament wanted the old faith under new rule. They killed some Protestants who attacked the faith, and they killed some Catholics who attacked the new rule. They even hanged a man for eating meat on Friday. But in general the changes were made without violence.

Henry's trust in parliament allowed the House of Commons to develop rapidly. During these busy years, its members gained experience which helped them to form good customs for the future. One of these customs demanded that the King should always listen to their complaints before they allowed his requests for money. If the council proposed bad laws, the House of Commons was ready to change them or to refuse them entirely. Its members were free from arrest, and speech was free, for Henry knew the value of sincere critics.

The House of Lords also made progress, for its church members no longer outnumbered the others. It often changed the Commons' laws or reduced their taxes. Acts of Parliament were printed and then sold in every village, so that all the people should know what was happening.

The only objections to the Reformation came from the north, where some of the abbeys still did good work among the poor. A rising of northern lords was quickly put down by an unpaid force of royal supporters. They were not against the King but they disliked the rough ways of his secretary, Thomas Cromwell, who was responsible for carrying out parliament's orders.

Henry kept no army, but he worked hard to provide defence for his island. He encouraged the villagers to learn how to shoot with guns instead of bows. He protected the southern ports with heavy guns. The navy was his special interest and he helped to plan a new type of battleship. The old kind of ship was good enough for the old kind of sea-fight, when they charged each other and their men fought hand-to-hand on board; but such ships did not suit Henry's new ideas of war at sea. Their length was only twice their breadth, which made them awkward to steer and hard to turn quickly in battle.

Instead of grouping the guns at each end, as the Spaniards did, Henry put them in a long row down each side. They fired through special holes in the ship's side, and the gunners were protected by the boards above them. This was the secret of English sea-power for the next three hundred years, and the empire could hardly have been won without it. The ships and guns, however, were only half the secret; the other half was their men. Most countries used sailors to sail their ships and soldiers to fight on them, with frequent quarrels between the two. But the English royal navy had a single service of fighting seamen.

Before Henry died he had built fifty-three of these new ships, with over 2,000 heavy guns on board. His navy was ready for battle.

Protestants being burnt

Archbishop Cranmer

I I

Protestants and Catholics

Mary I

Henry's family troubles did not end with his marriage to Ann Boleyn. She bore him a daughter, Elizabeth, but was unfaithful to her husband. After three years Henry cut off her head. His next wife, Jane Seymour, died in giving birth to his son Edward. His secretary Cromwell then brought him a foreign wife, Anne of Cleves, to please his German friends. Unfortunately she was neither well-educated nor beautiful. He sent her home, cut off Cromwell's head, and married a beautiful girl called Catherine Howard. But she too was unfaithful, so her head followed Cromwell's. His sixth and last wife, Catherine Parr, was a wise and gentle girl but she had no children.

By January 1547 Henry knew that his end was near. He appointed Protestant teachers to educate young Edward, and a mainly Protestant council to rule until Edward was old enough. This was not a sign that he specially favoured the Protestants. He had killed extreme Protestants as often as extreme Catholics. He wanted a moderate council to keep the peace between the two extremes, but he knew that the Catholic party were a greater danger to England's future independence. He died holding Cranmer's hand and was buried in his own church in Windsor Castle.

In spite of his trouble with his wives, Henry was a great king. His courage and political wisdom left England strong and free to make her way in a new world. She was no longer tied to Europe. Her wealth had passed from the dead hand of the feudal Church to men who would use it boldly for developing trade across the world.

While Henry lived he was able to control both Protestant and Catholic trouble-makers. But this policy could not last for ever; England had to make a choice. However, before she could do so she had to learn by bitter experience. For six years under the boy Edward she suffered from extreme Protestants. Then for five years under Mary she suffered from extreme Catholics. That was enough.

Edward VI was only fifteen when he died, so he cannot be blamed for the troubles of his time. At first his uncle, the Duke of Somerset, ruled for him. But Somerset was too mild to control the greedy men who began to seize the remaining property of churches and guilds, including their hospitals and schools. The guilds were not religious bodies, but their wealth was a temptation. The Duke of Northumberland killed Somerset and took his place, but he encouraged the greedy and scorned the poor. Extreme Protestants replaced all Catholic bishops and officials. Trade was in confusion. The cost of living went up and the value of money went down.

The only good memorial of these times is Cranmer's prayer-book. Its moderate treatment of the faith was welcomed on all sides, for it was a carefully chosen mixture of Catholic and Protestant material. It has given its own special religious flavour to the Anglican Church, which is still the official Church of England. But Cranmer, like Somerset, was too mild to control the extreme reformers.

When Edward died, the people welcomed his Catholic sister with open arms. But their joy did not last for long. Mary had grown up with a fierce hatred of those who had upset her mother's marriage. In four years she burnt three hundred Protestants. Some were great preachers like Bishops Latimer and Ridley. The gentle Cranmer was forced at first to sign a confession, but he changed his mind. As the fire rose round him he put out his right hand, which had signed the confession, and held it in the flames. But most of those who died were poor and humble people. Their deaths, said Latimer, lit a lamp which would never be put out.

Mary was determined to destroy all her father's work. First she put the Church back under the power of Rome. Then she married England's great enemy, King Philip of Spain, against the wishes of parliament. For three years Mary ruled under Spanish influence. Overseas trade was ruined since it was against Spanish interests. To please Spain, Mary made war on France; from this she gained nothing, but she lost Calais, the last English foothold on the mainland of Europe. It was a serious blow to national pride.

In 1558 Mary died. Her cruelty and her complete disregard for national feelings had destroyed any chance that the English people would ever again let the Roman Church control their affairs. Even her husband had grown tired of her, and had begun to take an interest in her Protestant sister, Elizabeth, who now became Queen.

Queen Elizabeth I

Map of the world in 1590

12

Elizabeth and Drake

The English had suffered so much under the rule of Mary that they did not expect anything better from her sister. They soon found that they were wrong. Elizabeth had many of her father's qualities, including good sense and strength of character. Like him, she understood her people. She loved hunting and dancing and gay entertainment. Many old inns and manors can boast truthfully that 'Queen Elizabeth slept here', for she often travelled round the country. She wanted to know her people and to be known by them.

'I know I have the body of a weak and feeble woman, but I have the heart of a king,' she told her army on one famous occasion, when Spain attempted to attack England. It was true, and the soldiers' cheers expressed the feelings of all her people.

Her soldiers and sailors admired her courage. Parliament respected her wisdom. The universities were astonished at her learning, for she could speak Latin and Greek as well as several modern languages. She once told parliament that, if she was driven out of the country with nothing but her underclothes, she could still earn her living anywhere in Europe. She enjoyed a joke. She never married but she used the threat of marriage as a political weapon.

Her chief minister, William Cecil, was an honest and far-seeing man who served her faithfully for forty years. With his help she quickly solved her first problem, the Church. Mary's cruelty had excited strong Protestant feeling, but most people wanted what her father had given them: a reformed Catholic Church that used the

English language and was free from foreign interference.

The Anglican Church under Elizabeth followed a middle course that satisfied all reasonable men; it also kept the loyalty of both Catholics and Protestants in time of danger. Its services were based on Cranmer's prayer-book. It encouraged men to study and to think. Gradually it became accepted as the true religious expression of the English renaissance; like Shakespeare's plays and Drake's adventures, it represented the spirit of the age.

Elizabeth's next problem was to keep her enemies quiet until her country was strong enough to defend itself. She had no doubt that Rome would encourage the Catholic kings of Europe to attack her, but she depended on the rivalry between France and Spain. She was sure that neither would let the other seize England.

France was the immediate danger since the French King had married Mary Stuart, the ruling Scottish Queen, and a French army was in control of Scotland. Mary was Elizabeth's nearest cousin and, if Elizabeth died without children, she could claim the English crown. On Cecil's advice, Elizabeth decided to interfere. With the help of her ships and soldiers, the Scottish Protestants were able to drive out the French. Eight years later, when Mary married the murderer of her second husband, she too was driven out and her son James became King instead.

Mary fled to England, where extreme Catholics soon made plans to make her Queen by murdering Elizabeth. Parliament angrily demanded her death, but Elizabeth was unwilling to kill her cousin. For eighteen years Mary was left in peace. Her supporters' plans were uncovered again and again by the watchful second minister, Walsingham; but the Queen refused to act, and she still allowed complete freedom to English Catholics. At last Walsingham seized Mary's private letters, which proved her knowledge of plans to murder the Queen. Philip of Spain had supported these plans, and when Mary's head was cut off he at once made preparations to attack England.

The Spaniards were almost ready to sail when a surprise attack by Sir Francis Drake destroyed all their ships in Cadiz harbour. Elizabeth still hoped to make peace by less violent means and she refused to let Drake repeat his attack next year. This was a mistake, for in July 1588 the great Armada of one hundred and thirty Spanish ships arrived quite unexpectedly in the Channel.

The navy was then commanded by Admiral Howard, with Drake as his second-in-command. Drake was playing a ball-game on the cliffs above Plymouth harbour when the Armada was seen approaching, and he refused to be disturbed. 'We have time to finish our game first and beat the Spaniards after,' he promised. And he kept his word.

The enemy had not planned an immediate attack. They wanted to collect their army in Belgium, which was under Spanish rule, and then carry it across to Kent. It was a simple plan but it had two serious faults. It depended on an armed rising by English Catholics, who in fact remained loyal; and it took no account of the English navy. Drake's guns had already broken the spirit of the enemy before they reached the shelter of Calais, for his fast ships could make circles round the slow and awkward Armada. Then the tide carried in his fire-ships, which drove the Spaniards back to sea in confusion. After a fierce battle they fled northwards without food or water, rather than risk a return journey through the Channel. At least fifty ships were wrecked on the Scottish and Irish coasts, and scarcely half the proud Armada managed to creep back to its home ports.

This defeat of Spain not only saved England but saved the Protestant faith in all northern Europe. A few years later an English force under Howard and Raleigh attacked Cadiz once more, destroyed the Spanish navy and seized its treasury. The Spanish threat to England had gone for ever.

The sailors who defeated the Armada were already accustomed to fighting Spaniards. For some sixty years they had been exploring the coasts of West Africa and of South America, where they were often attacked by Spanish forces. These English explorers were private merchant seamen, not soldiers, and their voyages were paid for by wealthy merchants at home who wanted trade, not war.

England's commercial policy in the sixteenth century had three aims. To find a quick way to India round the north of Russia or America; to trade peacefully with the colonies of other powers; and to find empty lands where she could plant her own colonies.

The first aim was not successful, though its results were valuable. The north-east passage led only to Archangel, but the ships' captains were welcomed in Moscow and opened a new Russian trade. The north-west passage led only to Canada, where later colonies developed a rich trade in fur. Meanwhile the second aim was hindered by Spanish jealousy. The Pope had given the whole un-explored world to Spain and Portugal, and Spain did not intend to share its riches with anyone. She even seized Portugal. The Spanish colonists themselves welcomed English trade, for their own govern-ment brought them nothing; it was only interested in the gold and silver from their mines. But their government's forces had orders to attack all strangers, and English prisoners were used as slaves to row Spanish ships.

Before long the English captains began to take their revenge. They attacked Spanish ships and seized their treasure. Even the cautious Cecil seized the Spanish army's pay-ships on the way to Belgium, though he discouraged interference overseas.

In 1577 Francis Drake set sail on a voyage round the world, which was sure to cause trouble with Spain. Cecil was against it but Walsingham was in favour, and on his advice Elizabeth not only gave her approval but secretly bought shares in the adventure. Drake sailed round the Cape and up the western coast of South America, where he took the Spanish colonies by surprise. He seized as much of their treasure as his ship could hold. Then he explored the coast of California and made his way across the Pacific and Indian Oceans, round Africa, and returned to England in 1580.

Drake was the first Englishman to sail round the world, and the success of his adventures had made him very popular in England. The Queen herself visited him on his ship, the *Golden Hind,* and laid her sword on his shoulder in the ancient ceremony by which knights are made. This royal recognition was of immense importance, for it encouraged the whole nation to build its future upon sea-power. The sea would not only be England's defence against her enemies in Europe: Drake had shown that it could also be used for exploration and trade in a wider world.

Our best record of the time is Hakluyt's *Voyages,* in which he describes his countrymen's many explorations. He mentions their trade with Persia, India and China, and recommends that all foreign trade should have the protection of the national flag. Elizabeth's government had not the means to give such official protection; instead they used the system of charter companies. A royal charter gave a company permission to make trading agreements with foreign rulers, to set up trading colonies, and to keep armed forces for their protection by land and sea.

The earliest companies covered West Africa, Russia, the Baltic Sea and the eastern Mediterranean; but the greatest of them all was the East India Company, which was formed in 1600 and later united all India. In empty or undeveloped lands around the world, trading colonies were set up which grew during the next three centuries into the British Empire; but the government never took over a colony until it was forced to do so by international problems. The first colony on the North American coast was Sir Walter Raleigh's Virginia, which was permanently settled in 1607. From here, twenty years earlier, he had returned with something that Europe had never seen before—tobacco.

An Elizabethan Family

The Nonesuch Palace

13

Shakespeare's England

An Elizabethan armchair

William Shakespeare had the good luck to grow up in a time of peace, when England was full of the new spirit of adventure. He had no religious troubles, for the Reformation was over; both Church and government reflected Elizabeth's courageous wisdom and the moderate influence of Cecil, her chief minister.

Shakespeare's plays are not merely exciting and amusing literature; they are a guide to Elizabethan life. Chaucer shows us how men in his time looked, talked and behaved. Shakespeare goes deeper; he shows us how the Elizabethans thought and felt. His astonishing knowledge of science and history and foreign lands reflects the influence of the Renaissance on English schools, for young William had a humble background and never went to university.

He was the son of a small trader in Stratford-on-Avon, where he attended the grammar school. We do not know what he learnt, but somehow his studies must have opened his eyes to the wonders of the world and of man's part in it. Later, in the private libraries of London friends like Lord Southampton, he would have had the chance to satisfy his curiosity.

In London he joined a company of actors, for which he wrote plays. This was then the most popular form of literature, though it was not printed and only actors had copies. Stories of love and war had replaced the religious subjects of earlier times. Like the plays of ancient Greece, they expressed the struggles of mankind in tears and laughter, love and hatred, beauty and fear. They were written by well-educated men like Udall, headmaster of Eton, and Christopher Marlowe. Rich nobles supported the companies of actors which performed in London's riverside theatres or toured the country manors. The actors were professional and the female parts were played by boys.

Although plays were only hand-copied, songs and music were printed for sale. Henry VIII and Elizabeth were both able musicians, and it was fashionable for young men to play and sing. English music, especially church music, was then among the best in Europe. It was fashionable, too, for great men to write poetry. Sir Walter Raleigh, sea-captain and explorer, even wrote a history of the world.

The arts were also favoured by the country squire, the small landowner who had replaced the feudal knight. He enjoyed hunting and sport, but he was also a well-educated farmer with a close interest in trade and exploration. He sent his sons to school and university, and had them trained for commerce or a profession. They were not allowed to idle at home. As J.P.s and M.P.s, the squires continued to serve their country as the knights had done. They were not paid for these services, and if they earned the rank of knight and called themselves 'Sir David' or 'Sir Anthony', it was a reward for public service rather than for service in war. But the country still depended largely on the middle-class yeoman farmer, who now owned the farm that he had formerly rented from an abbey or feudal lord.

Elizabethan houses were built for comfort and not for defence. Many of them are still lived in; not only fine manor-houses, but also simple cottages in old towns and villages. The squire's manor and the yeoman's farm-house are mostly of stone, sometimes taken from the ruins of an abbey. Red brick had been growing in popularity since Henry VI used it for his school at Eton; it was now in common use where stone was scarce, especially in the eastern counties. Some manors and most cottages have a wooden frame filled with bricks or clay, which may be covered with white plaster. The squire had pictures of his family on the walls, for these had been made popular by the court painter, Holbein. His rooms were comfortably furnished and lit by large glass windows.

Kent was already called the garden of England, because of its fruit farms. Foreign visitors noticed that more meat was eaten in England than in their own lands, where the animal population suffered from frequent wars. An Englishman, they said, could eat like a king, however humble his house might be. The rich still drank French wine, but beer (made from corn) was the common drink.

The heavy cavalry horses of the French wars were learning to work on the farms and pull the plough, and there was a demand for lighter riding-horses. Horse and cart carried local goods from town to town, but important trade still followed the rivers. Most of the four million people lived in the country, though the population of the city of London doubled itself to reach two hundred thousand under Elizabeth. It remained under middle-class control, for the great men built their houses west of the city, along the Strand or near the Queen at Westminster. York, Bristol and Norwich were large cities, but few other towns held more than five thousand people.

Ever since the Black Death, landowners had been enclosing farmland. When workers were scarce and wages were high, the only remedy was to keep sheep and cattle instead of growing corn. As the population increased again, this caused unemployment. Early Tudor governments tried to stop enclosure, but without success. Much feudal land came into the hands of yeomen farmers, who found enclosure the best way of controlling their animals. It led to more efficient farming, so that eighteenth-century governments even passed laws to enforce it.

The increase in cattle helped the leather industry, and the southern workers wore leather shoes while those in the north were still wearing wooden ones. The new glass industry supplied not only windows but bottles and drinking glasses, which formerly the rich had got from Italy. An English scientist, Roger Bacon, had invented special glasses for the eyes in the thirteenth century, and these were now useful for reading small print. New paper mills supplied the printers' own demands.

French and Italian clothing fashions were copied by the rich, who still wore a sword as part of their daily dress. Men of all classes wore beards. The inn was more than ever the social centre of each town and village. Here one could gather news of far-off places from travellers, whose numbers increased greatly when peace and order made the roads safe.

There was no class feeling, for the social system was in a state of gradual change. Feudal pride had gone, and the new educated classes had not yet learnt to look down on the simple worker. Any boy with brains and courage could win his way to a higher social standard. Every man who owned land or buildings worth forty shillings had the right to vote.

In the early years of the Reformation, problems of trade raised the cost of living and caused discontent in the countryside. Trouble with Spain and France was largely responsible, but the poor quality of English coins made things worse. Elizabeth replaced this weak money with new silver coins. She also set up a national control of wages and prices, workers' training, and trade in general. The guilds used to do this in the towns, but they had lost their power in recent years. Under the new law a boy of sixteen would have to be trained for seven years by his master, for 'until a man grows to twenty-three years he is usually wild, without enough experience to govern himself'. After that he could marry and set up his own business.

This system continued until the nineteenth century. It was a good one, for it provided industrial education under national control, and it solved the *school-leaver* problem more satisfactorily than we can do today. Strict rules governed the rights of both master and boy; the J.P.s were responsible for them and fixed local wage rates every year.

The laws also did much to balance the interests of town and country, of maker and market, of master and man. They encouraged the mining industry to increase production of tin, copper, lead and iron, which could provide modern weapons without depending on foreign supplies. They protected trees that were needed to build ships. Harbours were repaired. The old religious rule against eating meat on Fridays was extended to Wednesdays too, to help the fishing industry and thus train seamen for the navy. A customs-duty was placed on the import of things like knives, which were now being made in Sheffield; but skilled foreign workers in search of religious freedom were encouraged to come and settle.

The general aim was to avoid taxes and to develop a strong middle class which would perform the duties of defence and local government without payment. Only a small local tax was collected by the J.P.s to provide for the very poor, for whom they were responsible under the new Poor Law. This law forced members of a family to look after each other, but it helped to find work for the strong and to supply the weak with materials for home industry. It also provided cottages for homeless old people; many of these are still kept up with money which was given by landowners of those days. In matters like this, the Reformation was already influencing the nation's life. Rich men could no longer satisfy their consciences by leaving money to the Church; they began instead to make their own direct provision for the needs of the old, the homeless and the hungry.

In such a peaceful age crime was not a serious problem, and punishment was often more effective than it is now. For simple offences the criminal was usually fixed in a wooden frame in some public place, where everyone could laugh at him and small boys could practise their aim with a basketful of rotten fruit.

A seventeenth-century Scotsman

Caernarvon Castle in Wales

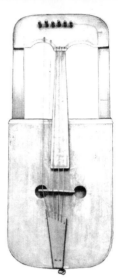

A crwth

14

The Story of Wales and Scotland

The words England and English (and the foreign forms Anglais, Inglés, Engelsk and so on) are commonly used nowadays to cover the lands and peoples of England, Scotland, Wales and even Ireland. This is confusing. Why does it happen? Why is this book called a *History of England*?

The island of Britain has three main parts. The part nearest the mainland of Europe was settled by the Romans, Anglo-Saxons, Danes and Normans, and it became known as England. The mountainous parts of the north and west were more easily defended, and remained unconquered; they became known as Scotland and Wales. The English language and the English forms of government were developed in England long before she became united with Wales (1535), Scotland (1707) or Ireland (1801). Even after union the English language spread only slowly, especially among country people, who may still use their own language today when talking among themselves.

In the eighteenth and nineteenth centuries the joint efforts of these peoples built the British Empire and played the leading part in developing the United States of America. Industrial progress also attracted thousands of Welsh, Scottish and Irish men to England, where they married English girls and settled down. Thus many *English* people today have mixed blood, but the pure Scot and the pure Welshman still live among their mountains.

In this chapter we will look at the story of Wales and Scotland, and in the next one we will consider the more difficult problem of

Ireland. There is no room here to tell all their history. This book aims to show how the England of King Alfred (who was writing English eight hundred years before union with Scotland) gradually developed into the United Kingdom that we know today. It is a *History of England* because England is the base on which the rest was built. The kingdom's common language has become such a powerful force that people everywhere speak of England and the English when they really mean Britain and the British.

William the Conqueror made no attempt to conquer Wales himself, but he divided the border lands between three great lords. Then he gave them permission to build castles and to seize as much of Wales as they could. They built their castles at the foot of each valley that led into the mountains. Most Welshmen were wandering sheep-farmers, and it was easy for them to escape when the Normans attacked. But through the ages they gradually settled in the valleys, accepted the rule of the lord in his castle, and traded in his markets.

The north-west part, round Mount Snowdon, remained under the Welsh royal family of Llewellyn, who accepted Henry II as their master. But a hundred years later they tried to break free and were defeated by Edward I. To prevent further trouble he built castles at Conway, Harlech and Caernarvon which are among the finest in the land. They were different from the simple Norman type, for they were surrounded by an outer wall that joined a number of small towers.

His first son was born in Caernarvon Castle and in 1301 he gave him the title of Prince of Wales, a title which is still given to the eldest son of the ruling king or queen. The Welsh taught Edward how to use their powerful weapon, the longbow. An arrow from this bow could go through a knight's armour and pin his leg to his horse's side. When Welsh soldiers joined the English army in the Hundred Years' War, their longbows played a decisive part in winning many battles.

Although all Wales was now ruled by the King of England, she was still separate from England, and local custom was mixed with English law. Early in the fourteenth century the Welsh leader Owen Glendower made a brave effort to win independence for his people. He failed, but Wales recovered her honour before long. Henry VII was a Welshman by birth and education, and he was proud of the arts and history of his people. Gradually he and Henry VIII brought peace and order to the land of their fathers. They personally owned most of the border lands, so it was not difficult to divide Wales into twelve counties and to organize local government on the English pattern. Welshmen were appointed J.P.s, and twenty-four Welsh representatives sat in parliament.

Now that a Welshman was wearing the English crown, the Welsh people accepted union. When Elizabeth became Queen, she had the Bible and prayer-book printed in their language, but they wisely kept out of the religious and political quarrels of the next two hundred years. Their Free Church began to open schools in every village to read the Bible, but education did not change their ways. They remained content with the life of their farms and coal-mines; unlike the Scots and the Irish, few Welshmen left home to try their fortune in the colonies.

Today there is a full-time radio service in Welsh, which is widely used as a second language. The Welsh are especially fond of singing. In the yearly *Eisteddfod* they gather together to enjoy the songs, the poetry and the music of their country.

The Roman Emperor Hadrian built a wall which runs across north England from Carlisle to Newcastle. It was intended to keep out the wild Scottish tribes. The Saxons crossed this wall and took possession of Northumberland. Their new border ran roughly from Carlisle to the River Tweed, as it does today.

Another Roman emperor built a wall across the narrowest part of Scotland which separates the highlands from the lowlands. These two halves of the land still reflect the differences of a thousand years of history. The highlands were always fiercely independent and resisted the influences of English civilization. As a result their country remains the most unspoilt, the most beautiful, and the poorest part of the island. The lowlands, however, have played a part in English history since the days of Macbeth, whose name has been made famous by Shakespeare's play.

When King Duncan of Scotland was killed by Macbeth, his young son Malcolm escaped to England, where he was given a friendly welcome. Seventeen years later, in 1057, he drove out his father's murderer with English help. He then welcomed many English families who escaped the Norman conquest and settled in the lowlands, where their language quickly spread. His sons realised that the only way to keep out the Normans was to adopt their feudal system of defence; so they invited Norman knights across the border and gave them lands. These knights built castles and ruled the countryside with their cavalry. They became loyal Scots, and some of their names, like Balliol, Bruce and Wallace, are among the most famous in Scottish history. Parish churches, abbeys and cathedrals soon reflected the English religion; the county system, royal courts and borough charters reflected English government. Slowly this influence spread over all the lowlands.

In 1286 the crown passed to Margaret, the daughter of the King of Norway. Arrangements were made for her to marry the eldest son of Edward I, which would have united the kingdoms of England and Scotland. But her ship was wrecked on the way from Norway and she was drowned. Edward now supported the claim of her cousin, John Balliol, whose father had built Balliol College at Oxford to house Scottish students.

The new king was at first grateful for Edward's support, but he soon found that he had little real power. When he tried to act independently, Edward seized him and took him to London. Edward also took the ceremonial stone on which all kings of Scotland were crowned, and placed it under the royal chair in Westminster Abbey. There it still lies. But Scotland would not suffer such treatment for long, and her spirit was stirred by two great leaders, William Wallace and Robert Bruce. It was Bruce who defeated a much larger English force under Edward II in the great Scottish victory of Bannockburn in 1314.

For the next two hundred years Scotland remained free but desperately poor. Her friendship with France brought her no profit but frequent border wars. Universities were opened at St. Andrews, Glasgow and Aberdeen, but education without commerce could not raise the standard of living. Only union with England could bring commercial progress.

In 1513 the English took their revenge for Bannockburn; at the battle of Flodden the King of Scotland was killed with many of his noblemen and ten thousand of his soldiers. Catholic church leaders then held power until they married their young Queen Mary to the King of France, and a French army took control of Scotland. This was more than national pride could bear. A rising was led by the Protestant preacher John Knox, who was supported by most of the remaining noblemen. With Elizabeth's help they drove out the French and gained control of the weak parliament in Edinburgh. Then, like Henry VIII, they cut all ties with Rome.

We already know what happened to Mary. Her son James was only one year old when he was crowned in Edinburgh, but he grew up with the firm intention of being crowned in London too. With this object, he did his best to follow Elizabeth's religious policy and to keep extreme Protestants under control. He brought peace and order to the countryside, and made the highland chiefs responsible for their people.

The Scottish social system is based on the clan, which is an extended family group. The Campbell clan, for example, covers the county of Argyll, and the Duke of Argyll is their clan chief. The national dress for both men and women includes a kind of skirt called a kilt, which is woven with a different pattern for each clan. Times change and the kilt is not now worn so much, except for ceremonies and in the army; but every true Scot is still proud of his clan.

When Elizabeth died, the English parliament accepted James as their King; but they were not yet ready for political union with such a poor and unsettled country as Scotland. For another century the two countries remained separate, though loyalty to the crown brought peace and encouraged trade between them. Scotland profited so greatly by this arrangement that in 1707 she agreed to complete union under the parliament at Westminster, whoever England's future kings might be.

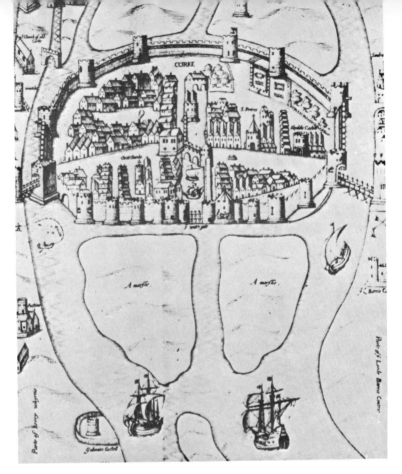

A map of Cork in 1633

*The inauguration of an Irish King from
a twelfth-century manuscript*

15

The Story of Ireland

A harp

Ireland had not been troubled by the Romans or Saxons, though Danes had settled on the east coast and built towns like Dublin. The Irish themselves had no towns; each man lived on his farm and passed his days happily in raising his own cattle or stealing his neighbours'. They were simple people who only wanted to be left in peace.

They were too simple, in fact, to resist either the greed of the feudal ages or the heartless politics of modern times. St. Patrick had brought them Christianity in the fifth century, but they were not united in Church or State. Their clan system was not so well organized as in Scotland, though even today one finds that many people in a district seem to have the same name. Thus they were defenceless against the private army of Norman cavalry and Welsh longbowmen who seized the land in 1169. The leaders of this army were border lords who had mixed with the Welsh and so had no difficulty in settling down among the Celtic Irish.

King Henry II then took official possession of the island. The Danes were driven out and Dublin was given to the citizens of Bristol; its castle became the seat of government until the twentieth century. The district around Dublin came under direct royal rule. The rest of the island remained under Irish clan chiefs in the west and under Normans in the east, but these soon married Irish girls and lost touch with their own people.

For a while there was peaceful development. Dublin and Cork became busy ports. After Bannockburn, the victorious Scots landed

93

in the north and took possession of the Ulster district, but England was too busy with her wars to attend to Irish affairs for the next two centuries. Her language and civilization were unknown in Ireland beyond Dublin.

Henry VIII did not understand the Irish. He did not realize that the new learning of the Renaissance had never reached them; that the Catholic Church was still popular and socially useful; that its abbeys had no wealth which he could use to keep their schools going. His interference with the Church in Ireland was a mistake for which both countries have suffered ever since. All Ireland except Ulster was now united in loyalty to Rome and in hatred of England.

Henry tried to fit the clan chiefs into a new system of government. This might have been possible before the Reformation, but in the heat of religious quarrels it was hopeless. The violent extremes of Edward and Mary only made things worse, so that Elizabeth was faced with a serious problem. The southern Irish were especially friendly with Spain, and she realized that Spain could easily take the island and use it as a base for attack on England.

Peaceful agreement was clearly necessary to solve this problem, but no such agreement was ever reached. Spanish armies twice landed in Ireland and were destroyed by Elizabeth's forces. To guard against this danger she colonized all the south with Englishmen, who were given land for settlement. She also opened a university in Dublin and encouraged education. Meanwhile thousands of Protestant Scots were settling in Ulster to escape the rule of James.

In the seventeenth-century quarrel between King and Parliament, Catholic Ireland supported the King, but it was defeated and severely punished. The whole island was handed over to Protestant settlers, except for the parts west of the River Shannon. The eighteenth century passed peacefully, but Napoleon's wars raised the old problem of defence. This led to the union of the two islands in 1801 under one parliament at Westminster, where Irish members joined those of Wales and Scotland. But parliament was still blinded by religious prejudice and failed to reach any fair solution to Irish problems. In the end, Catholic Ireland became an independent country, called Eire; but Protestant Ulster chose to remain part of the United Kingdom.

In spite of everything, the ties of blood and language still hold Eire close to Britain, where she is regarded as a sister country rather than a foreign one.

Oliver Cromwell dismissing the Long Parliament

Guy Fawkes and his friends

16

King against Parliament

A cavalier

James Stuart had already been King of Scotland for thirty-six years when he became King of England too. The English accepted him because they wanted peace with their northern neighbours and he was the only direct descendant of the Tudors. He knew nothing of English law or custom, and he was too proud to listen to advice. He believed that kings were responsible only to God and not to any parliament. There had not been a proper parliament in Scotland, so he could not understand it when the House of Commons refused his demands for tax and talked of laws. In his view, the King's will was the only law.

His cousin Elizabeth's wisdom had kept the balance of religion, trade and foreign affairs. James was an unwise king, who hoped to keep the same balance by his royal word alone. His hopes were soon proved false. The extreme Catholics were disappointed by his moderate views and they decided on violent action. They planned to blow up the whole of parliament, and the King with it, on November 5th, 1605.

At the last moment one of them told their secret in order to save the lives of his Catholic cousins in the House of Lords. A search was made under the parliament buildings, and a man called Guy Fawkes was found with matches in his hand and a barrel of gunpowder at his side. All moderate opinion was silenced by this attempt at mass-murder, and Catholics were forbidden to enter the public service or any profession. November 5th is still called Guy Fawkes Day, and a figure representing him (made of old clothes filled with straw) is ceremonially burnt in every village.

James left most government business in the hands of favourites like the Duke of Buckingham. He scorned the House of Commons and had no minister among its members. As a result of this neglect, it produced its own independent leaders and became a more powerful body than it had been when Tudor ministers controlled its discussions. The Lords disliked James, for he began to sell titles for money. London disliked him too, for he discouraged the merchant explorers, though his peace with Spain protected trade at home; he also married his son Charles to the Catholic daughter of the King of France.

Young Charles had a stronger character than his father, but he was an equally bad judge of men. He depended on his father's favourite, Buckingham, who brought him into violent disagreement with parliament. Was the law above the King, or the King above the law? It was a simple question, but in the end it cost Charles his life.

First he dismissed parliament, and for eleven years he tried to rule without it. Under his wife's influence he took Catholics as his ministers, and William Laud, who had Catholic sympathies, was appointed Archbishop of Canterbury. Thousands of Protestants sailed to America every year to escape. Honest judges were dismissed, and trouble was bound to come. Surprisingly, it did not come at first from the English but from the King's own Scottish countrymen. For Charles and his friend Lord Strafford tried to raise an Irish Catholic army to put down a Protestant rising in Scotland and in northern Ireland, which had a large Scottish population. Then he recalled parliament from its long rest and demanded money to pay this unwelcome force. Parliament refused, and when a Scottish army crossed the border, the English refused to fight them. Charles called parliament once more, and this time he had to listen to their complaints before they would consider his request for money.

The leaders of the Commons were Pym, Hampden and Oliver Cromwell, who was a descendant of Henry VIII's unpopular secretary. They were bold men, and while the Scottish army threatened the King they could do what they pleased. The Lords supported them and arrested Strafford, whose head was cut off.

The royal court of the Star Chamber was closed, for it had been used unfairly against the King's personal enemies. All taxes were declared unlawful unless they received parliament's approval, for Charles had been acting against the rules of Magna Carta. In future the King could not dismiss parliament until it was ready to go, and he had to call it every three years at least. All this was useful, but it still let the King refuse parliament's laws; it also let him take direct action without asking its opinion.

The Commons now seized the opportunity of attacking the archbishop and the Catholic ministers, who clearly wanted to bring back the power of Rome. They also demanded control of the armed forces, which law and custom had always placed under the King. This was a difficult point, and the Lords wanted time to discuss it. But Charles was in a hurry, and the Queen persuaded him to take violent action. He went to the House of Commons with several hundred soldiers to arrest its leaders; but they had already escaped by water to the city, where they were safe.

All London was now arming itself to defend parliament against such royal interference. Charles escaped to the north, and parliament sent him their demands. They wanted control of the army, control of the appointment of judges and ministers, and a more Protestant religious policy. Charles refused.

The war which followed was not a class war. Most members of parliament were squires, and they were supported by at least half the land-owning class; by the older noble families; by most merchants and boroughs; by the navy and the merchant seamen; and by most of the south and east of England. The printing presses, the treasury and the arms stores were in their hands. The navy could prevent Charles from receiving any help from Europe.

The supporters of parliament were called Roundheads by their enemies because the common people of London kept their hair cut very short. They in turn called the King's men Cavaliers, which meant 'proud, upper-class horsemen'; but the King was widely supported by all classes in the north and west. Some were Catholic; others were influenced by the Englishman's natural distrust of politicians and his natural respect for the Crown. Most land-owners on the King's side owed their titles to his father, who had appointed over two thousand knights as well as forty lords. Families were often divided, and each man followed his own conscience. But most of the common people refused to take sides at all.

Charles made Oxford his base, but it had none of the advantages of London. His nephew Rupert was a good cavalry leader, but Oliver Cromwell was a better one. After three years of struggle, the King's forces were destroyed at the battle of Naseby by Cromwell's well-disciplined men. The King himself escaped to the Scottish highlands but he was taken prisoner two years later.

By this time parliament's two great leaders, Pym and Hampden, were dead. Without them the Commons quarrelled among themselves, failed to pay their army, and refused complete religious freedom to their extreme Protestant supporters. Charles still would not accept their demands, for he hoped that the quarrel between parliament and the army would help his cause. Many members were anxious to arrange a settlement, but the army was rapidly losing patience with them. Now its generals marched to London, seized money to pay their men, and took control of parliament. They had to set up a special court to try the King, for no judge would take part in such an unlawful act. Even then, less than half the court would agree to sign an order for the King's death, which the generals demanded.

King Charles's head was cut off in Whitehall in January 1649 and he was buried at Windsor beside Henry VIII. Popular feeling was against his unjust trial, and many of his enemies were angry and ashamed at his death. He was, in spite of his faults, the King, and few people had any feeling of loyalty to the 'preaching generals' of the Protestant army.

Cromwell's council now had many enemies, and he did not dare to hold elections. The colonies and all Europe turned against him, but he had the courage to finish what he had begun. His well-trained army quickly took control of Scotland and Ireland. His navy under Admiral Blake defeated the French, the Spaniards and the Dutch, and brought the colonies under his rule; it even protected merchant ships in the Mediterranean, which no English warship had ever entered before. Its two hundred ships developed bold new methods of attack, and it became a regular profession with improved service conditions. But the country could not afford to keep such large forces for long.

Meanwhile the House of Lords had been closed, and the extreme Protestants had been making themselves rich by stealing the land and property of their enemies. But trade was bad, and the common people were tired of the costs of war. They also thoroughly disliked the new government's strict ideas on morality. Theatres and drinking-houses were closed. Horse-racing was forbidden. It was an offence to swear, or to travel on Sundays. A man could be put to death for immorality with his neighbour's wife, though in fact no jury would let this happen. The new church leaders preached a religion of holy misery; 'pleasure is sin' was their cry, and even the feast of Christmas was forbidden because it made men happy. The working man remembered sadly the good old days, when Sunday afternoon meant football and merry dancing on the village green.

Cromwell soon quarrelled with parliament. He marched into the House of Commons with his red-coated soldiers and drove its members out into the street. Then he took personal control of government. He divided the country into eleven districts and ruled through a group of generals with their own local armies. It was efficient government, but the people hated it.

When Cromwell died there was no one to take his place. The country was ready to welcome any leader who could bring back normal government. General Monk, the commander of the army in Scotland, was such a leader. He arranged free elections for a new parliament, which promptly decided to bring back the rule of kings. Just eleven years after Charles I's death cheering crowds welcomed back his son as Charles II, and all the bells of London rang with joy.

A seventeenth-century fire engine

William III

17

The Settlement of 1689 and the Treaty of Utrecht

The battle of Ramillies

Charles II was lucky to have a wise chief minister, Lord Clarendon, who now worked hard to make peace between the two sides. Only ten Roundheads, who had signed the order for Charles I's death, were killed. Everyone else was forgiven. The Cavaliers got back the lands that their enemies had seized; but they did not get back what they had been forced to sell, and this made them very angry. They had most of the seats in the new parliament and they used this power to take revenge on their enemies.

They would not let any Roundhead work in local government, or as a priest or schoolmaster, unless he belonged to the Anglican Church. This was the official Church once more, but many Roundheads preferred to support the Free Church, which was not under parliament's control. The Cavaliers also decided that the King should command the armed forces, though parliament would control their numbers. They dismissed most of Cromwell's army but they kept the royal horse guards; these still guard the Queen today when she drives through London on State occasions. Most Cavaliers placed their trust in the county reserves rather than in the professional forces, which included many hired foreigners.

Charles himself was a good-natured man, very different from his proud father. He had many love affairs, the most famous being with the actress Nell Gwyn. But he married the daughter of the King of Portugal, who gave him Tangier and Bombay as a present to mark the occasion.

He loved the navy and was keen on trade and colonization. He supported the new Royal Society for the advance of science, which encouraged scientific study in every field. One of its first members was Sir Christopher Wren, who soon had the chance to prove his skill. In 1666 a great fire destroyed a large part of the city, and Wren helped to build a new London on the burnt ruins. His buildings included St. Paul's Cathedral and over fifty churches. The exchange of members' ideas was helped by a new weekly postal service between London and important towns.

Charles allowed freedom of the press and did his best to work with parliament; but suddenly everything went wrong. A terrible disease, like the Black Death of the fourteenth century, killed seventy thousand London citizens. In the following year the great fire broke out. Trade was ruined. There was no money to pay the navy, and its ships were tied up at Chatham until a Dutch force sailed in and destroyed them.

The country now blamed the King's friendship with France for all its troubles. Clarendon was driven from office. Even Charles at last realized that France was planning to seize Holland and control the Rhine. In such a position she could threaten not only England but all Protestant Europe. The situation was the same as in 1588, when Spain had been the enemy; it was repeated by Napoleon in 1793 and by the Germans in 1914. England could not afford to let either Holland or Belgium fall into the hands of the greatest power in Europe.

Charles was now thoroughly frightened and turned to parliament for support. By this time the Cavaliers and Roundheads had settled down to become England's first political parties, the Tories and the Whigs. Charles made friends with the Tory party; on their advice he married his brother's daughter Mary to his nephew William, the ruler of Holland. The Whigs were still not satisfied and began to stir up popular feeling against the King's brother, James, who was a Catholic and was likely to be the next king. Most people did not want a Catholic king, but the Whigs' violent behaviour reminded England too much of Cromwell. Some of them were caught planning to murder the King and his brother on the way back from Newmarket races, and this broke up the party leadership.

Then Charles died, and the extreme Whigs led a rising in support of the Protestant Duke of Monmouth, who was Charles's son but not the Queen's. The rising was quickly put down by the new King, James II, but his revenge destroyed all the sympathy that he had won. His friend Judge Jeffreys is remembered as the cruellest man in England's history, for he then hanged and burned three hundred people and sent a thousand more to work as slaves on American farms.

James unwisely decided to keep the army that had been raised against Monmouth, and to use it for his own purposes. His clear aim was to put Catholics in control of the army, the Church, the courts, and all central and local government. But he failed to understand that the English Catholics did not want their religion to be forced upon the country; they only wanted to be given their full rights as citizens.

After three years of struggle, the Whig and Tory leaders were at last united against him. William of Holland landed with an army at their invitation, and he was so warmly welcomed that James ran away to France without any attempt at resistance. William and Mary were then crowned as joint rulers.

The events of 1689 settled the religious and political problems for the next hundred and fifty years. The religious settlement may seem one-sided to us, but then it seemed fair and reasonable. Only members of the Anglican Church could attend a university or hold any public office, and no Catholic could sit in parliament. It was a victory for moderate men against those who held extreme views, whether Catholic or Protestant. The King and parliament were no longer rivals. They worked together, as they had in Henry VIII's time, but now parliament was the stronger power.

The problem of the royal house also had to be settled, for James or his Catholic son might try to return if Mary died childless. It was decided that the crown should pass first to Mary's sister Anne and then to a distant cousin in the royal house of Hanover, which was a north German state. It was also decided that no future king or queen could be a Catholic. Meanwhile Scotland accepted William and Mary, and under Anne the two countries were at last united under the parliament of Westminster.

The troubles of the royal family of Stuart were caused mainly by the influence of France and Spain, whose rulers regarded

Protestant England as a dangerous example to their own people. It was clear that her trade could never develop until these two countries learned to leave her in peace.

The old Spanish threat to Europe's freedom had been destroyed by the defeat of the Armada, but the new French threat could not be dealt with quite so easily. France was a powerful country with a large population, and her central position made her a good base for attacking her neighbours. Thus the eighteenth century opened with a war in which England, Holland, Austria, Portugal, Denmark and most German states were allies (countries united for war) against France, Spain and the state of Bavaria.

It was not a religious war, for even the Pope was anxious about French ambitions and preferred to see a balance of power in Europe. A Protestant England suited him better than an England under French influence; and half her allies were Catholic anyhow. These allies were now led to victory by John Churchill, Duke of Marlborough, with a determination that was worthy of his famous descendant, Winston Churchill.

Marlborough was not only a great leader in battle but a great organizer. His supplies were always ready in advance: food and money, new shoes, even bridges of boats for crossing rivers by surprise. He understood the value of naval support and the need to keep allies happy. He understood politicians too, and would not let their quarrels interfere with his skilled management of the war. The English and Dutch navies first drove the enemy out of the Channel, then seized Gibraltar and took control of the Mediterranean. When the French left the safety of their border castles to attack Austria, Marlborough saw his chance to catch them off their guard. Speed was essential. He knew that the government would not agree to his plans, so he did not tell it. He hurried his allied army across the Rhine and down to the Danube, where he won a great victory at Blenheim. Another victory at Ramillies drove the French out of Belgium and Holland.

In both these battles the cavalry were decisive, but the foot-soldier's value was doubled by the use of the bayonet, which is a long knife fixed to the end of a gun. The costs of war were high but parliament gladly paid, for they knew that England's future depended on it. They were not now fighting for some ancient Norman claim; they were fighting for the right to trade wherever they pleased, without foreign interference. The charter companies and the newly-formed Bank of England realized this and gave all the help they could.

The Treaty of Utrecht in 1713 brought peace. A treaty is an international agreement, and Spain agreed that England should keep Gibraltar 'absolutely and for ever' as a naval base, to protect her trade. France agreed to give up claims to various parts of Canada and to hand over Belgium to Austria, which seemed a safe arrangement to the English.

An eighteenth-century meal

Prior Park near Bath

18

Eighteenth-century Society

An eighteenth-century clock

Queen Anne died in the year after Utrecht, and the crown passed to her cousin George of Hanover, who was a great-grandson of James I. He spoke no English; but he was a Protestant, he hated the French, and his forces had helped with Marlborough's wars. These were strong points in his favour. His lack of English even turned out to be a blessing. It prevented him from holding council and so led to the *cabinet* system of government. The cabinet is a council which contains the leaders of the biggest party in parliament, and its chief is called the Prime Minister. The members of a cabinet must agree on common aims and they must take joint responsibility for all that they do.

The first real prime minister was Robert Walpole, who gradually developed this system during twenty-one years in office. The English form of government has never been fixed in writing. It has slowly taken shape through the experience of centuries, but a few men like Walpole have left their personal mark upon it.

Walpole led the Whig party, but he understood the Tories. His plan was 'to let sleeping dogs lie': to do nothing that would stir up trouble. He was not a coward, but he knew that his country needed long years of peace to build up its strength. He was a man of kindness and common sense, like Elizabeth's chief minister, Cecil. He had no desire for personal glory.

Under Walpole's leadership the English had complete freedom of speech and of person, such as no other country had. They knew it and were proud of it. They liked a government that let hard-working men develop trade and agriculture without official inter-ference. Eighteenth-century England grew strong and healthy through the uncontrolled efforts of her people. The State had no need to interfere until industrial progress demanded reforms in local government. In the meanwhile the Whig party ruled the land in peace.

The cost of Marlborough's wars was partly paid by a land tax, which Walpole kept in force. It did not worry the Whigs, who mostly owned enough land to give them an honoured position in society but were not dependent on it. It did seriously worry the Tory squire, who depended on his land for his living. Because of the land tax, he was often forced to sell his property to some large landowner. However, he was usually able to rent it and remain in possession. This was fortunate, for the squire knew every family in his village and took a personal interest in their lives. He continued to do so till the present century, when the State took over his responsibilities.

In spite of taxes, the squire led a busy but comfortable life. He sat in court as an unpaid J.P., he ran his farms, he hunted and fished. He had to keep his accounts with more care, but he could afford to raise a large family. The sons of the rich might go to the big public schools, but a local grammar school was usually good enough for his. If possible, some parents preferred to keep their sons at home with a private teacher, who was often a Frenchman. He could teach things that were not taught in school: French and Italian, natural history, accounts, drawing, dancing and sword-play.

Most squires were interested in the arts and liked to fill their houses with books and paintings. Their tastes encouraged a new artistic standard of manufacture—Chippendale's light and graceful furniture, and delightful cups and plates that Josiah Wedgwood made from the white clay of Cornwall.

The King's court no longer led society, for George I and George II were not accustomed to English ways, though George II learnt to speak English. The gap was filled by a young man called Beau Nash, who ruled polite society from his meeting-rooms in Bath. Here fashionable people gathered to take the health-giving waters, which had been famous since Roman days.

Nash organized dances and social parties, where everyone had to follow his strict rules of behaviour. Even the upper classes still had rough habits, and gentlemen were accustomed to settle their quarrels with the sword; but Nash would not allow swords or travelling clothes in his rooms. Gentlemen had to be neatly dressed and they were forbidden to smoke or swear in front of ladies. As Master of Ceremonies at Bath he taught polite manners to the land-owning and merchant classes for half a century; his influence was still felt long after his death, as Dickens so amusingly describes in *Pickwick Papers*.

New streets of fine houses were built for his visitors, which made Bath the grandest city outside London. They also learnt to enjoy the works of Handel, who left Germany as a young man and settled in England to write his music.

The English were the first tourists, and every rich young gentleman was sent on a tour of Europe to complete his education. He took his own carriage and servants, and for a year he travelled to Paris, Vienna, Venice and other centres of civilization. Especially he liked Italy, where the sun shone even in the winter; from here he brought back to England works of art and new ideas of building.

The Tudor house has all the qualities that an Englishman connects with the word *home*. It has a warm and friendly look. It fits quietly into its surroundings. Its rooms are comfortable but not too large; they were planned for the family. But the Georgian house is a grander affair altogether, and it stands out boldly against its surroundings. Its rooms are large, and it expects to entertain society with parties and dances; but its grand appearance is based on the simple lines and balanced measurements of ancient Rome.

In England men could now travel for pleasure, for roads were much improved. The parishes had always taken care of their local roads, but no one had really troubled about the highways since Roman times. The State could not afford to do anything, but the new type of businessman had an easy solution to the problem. He formed private companies to keep the roads in good repair, and money was collected from all who passed their gates. New bridges were paid for in the same way.

The immense industrial and agricultural development of the Georgian age would not have been possible without good roads and waterways. The Duke of Bridgewater built the first canals to carry coal from his mines to Manchester. Soon private companies were building them to connect all the great rivers between London, Liverpool, Bristol and Hull. The canals also improved housing conditions for the poor, as they carried building materials cheaply to the growing towns.

The rich had their own carriages, but anyone could travel by the public ones, called stage-coaches, which ran between the towns. These were drawn by four or six horses but they had no springs, so they were not very comfortable. Special inns along the roads provided fresh horses for each stage of the journey, and this accounts for the name *stage*-coach.

Better farming kept most of the people well fed, especially in the country. Bread, butter, cheese and meat were cheap and plentiful. Women and children began to drink Indian tea instead of beer. Foreign visitors remarked (as they still do) that the English had good food but did not know how to cook it. The great French writer Voltaire complained that 'the English have a hundred religions but only one sauce'. A German student wrote home that the meat at his lodgings was only half cooked, 'but there is a kind of bread-and-butter which is roasted by the fire on a fork. It is called toast and is extremely good.'

Cricket was already becoming the English national game. The village green was its home, but by mid-century an all-England eleven was playing matches against the counties. Horse-racing, 'the sport of kings and king of sports', drew large crowds to its meetings, especially at Newmarket, where the best horses in the land took part. The theatre also provided popular entertainment, not only in London but in the market towns where companies of players were formed. Shakespeare's work still ruled the stage, but the spirit of the times has been passed down to us in plays like Sheridan's *The School for Scandal*.

On the whole, country people were fairly contented, especially when the local squire took a real interest in them. But in London the poor had no squire to look after them. They lived in the back streets of the city, or out on the east side of the walls where the ships were tied. They wasted their money on card games and on drinking gin, for this strong spirit was cheap. A man could be hanged for stealing five shillings; but there were no police to catch him, and crime was on the increase. Even in London, however, the efforts of private men provided remedies. They forced the government to put a tax on gin. They arranged for fatherless children to be taken to country homes and taught a trade. They built hospitals. The various Churches stopped quarrelling about their beliefs and became rivals in the field of education instead. They opened free schools to teach reading, writing and religion, to clothe their children, and to help them to find good employers. Cheap Bibles and prayer-books were printed for them. The brothers Charles and John Wesley, who started the Methodist Church, were especially active in this work.

The Bible was usually the poor man's only book, but several hundred companies were producing literature for the entertainment of the middle classes. The powerful figure of Samuel Johnson stands out among all the writers of that age, for his dictionary set a standard for the proper use and spelling of the language. His life story by Boswell was based on daily notes of his sayings and doings; so his strange habits are as familiar to us as they were to his friends in the coffee-houses.

These coffee-houses were the centre of London's social life. Here men with common interests could meet, for private clubs had not yet become the fashion. Whatever a man's views were on politics or religion, on art or sport, there was a coffee-house to suit his tastes. Edward Lloyd's coffee-house attracted everyone who was interested in overseas trade. The newspapers did not report commercial affairs or the movement of ships, but at Lloyd's you could learn the latest news of them from everywhere. Today the association that bears his name is world-famous, particularly for the insurance of ships and for the daily report of the movement of ships at every port in the world.

The growth of overseas trade resulted from new methods of farming and manufacture at home. New root-crops made it possible to fatten cattle in winter, and parliament began to force the enclosure of common land that was being wastefully used. This was hard on the small farmer; but growing towns had to be fed and only big farms could supply their needs.

Meanwhile young engineers were inventing machines that attracted more workers into industry. Steam-pumps were used in the mines. Cotton mills used new machinery that was driven by water-power. Gradually the population was moving north to the riverside mills of Lancashire and Yorkshire. The British were about to become Europe's first industrial nation.

*Captain Cook's ship, Endeavour, being
repaired*

*'The spirit of 76', the American War
of Independence*

19

The Start of an Empire

William Pitt

While England was gathering strength at home, Walpole's government resisted demands for a new war against France and Spain. In spite of the Treaty of Utrecht, these two countries were still interfering with foreign trade. The 'war of Jenkin's ear' was forced on the government after a Spanish official had torn off the ear of that unfortunate sea-captain. It was followed by more serious fighting which spread from France to India and Canada. There were also far-reaching effects in Scotland.

James II's son had made an unsuccessful attempt to seize England with a highland army on Queen Anne's death. In 1745 his grandson, the gay and good-looking Prince Charles, was persuaded by the French to try again. The English army was busy in France, and Charles marched half-way to London before he was driven back. His highland friends fought bravely; but he got little support from the rest of Scotland, which was already profiting from free trade with England and her colonies.

The rising was severely punished, and the ancient feudal rule of the highland chiefs was brought to an end. Their lands were at last opened to trade, and education could spread. It was a difficult time, as Stevenson's *Kidnapped* shows us, but it brought Scotland into the world of commerce and exploration. Her men soon took an active part in every field of Britain's development; from this time, we can speak of Britain as a country, not merely as an island. In the field of literature Scotland now produced two of her best-known writers, Robert Burns and Sir Walter Scott.

Meanwhile, the fighting skill of the highland soldiers was now valuable to Britain in her wars abroad. France was causing trouble for the colonies in America. These colonies stretched along the coast from the St. Lawrence river down to Spanish Florida, and they were gradually spreading inland. To prevent this westward spread, the French Canadians built a line of strongly armed posts; they ran from the Great Lakes down the Ohio and Mississippi rivers to New Orleans.

At first the French had it all their own way, while British politicians quarrelled endlessly among themselves. Then at last one powerful minister took charge. His name was William Pitt and he later became Lord Chatham; we shall call him Chatham to distinguish him from his equally famous son, the younger William Pitt.

The success of the years 1757–59 was Chatham's personal victory. His powerful speeches united parliament and the nation. He chose good commanders, gave them the right orders, and provided the right forces. He knew how to combine the army and the navy into a joint war-machine. He repeated Marlborough's efficiency on a world-wide scale.

First he arranged with George II's nephew, Frederick of Prussia, to keep the French busy in Europe while he dealt with their armies overseas. The Scottish highlanders helped the American colonists to drive them out of the Ohio valley; the navy took General Wolfe's little force up the St. Lawrence River to attack their base at Quebec. Here the French had perfect natural defences. But one dark night Wolfe led his men by a secret path up a steep cliff, and at daybreak they took the enemy by surprise. Quebec fell, and within a year all French resistance in Canada was over.

Meanwhile in India the French had attempted to destroy the East India Company. They were defeated at Plassey by the company's forces under Robert Clive, who became the first Governor of Bengal. For the next fifty years they continued to stir up trouble, and their officers led risings against the company. But each occasion resulted in an extension of the company's influence, which soon spread to the upper Ganges and all south India.

The American colonies remained loyal to Britain while they needed her protection; but when the French threat was no longer there, this loyalty weakened. They had never accepted the right of

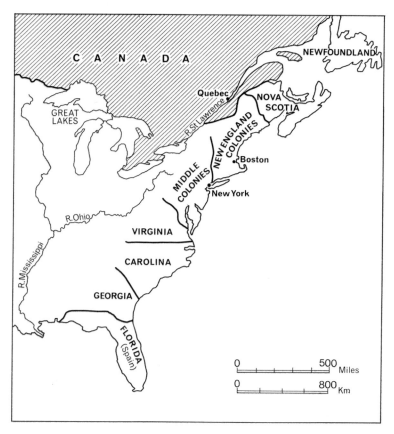

North American Colonies in 1780, with Canada shaded

parliament to make laws for them or to tax them. Each was ruled by its own elected council, which was responsible to the King through his local governor. But there was no political unity, and conditions varied according to their various origins.

The southern colonies of Virginia, Carolina and Georgia had been developed by merchants for their cotton and tobacco. The planters needed a large number of workers; they welcomed African slaves, but they also used criminals from Britain.

The middle colonies, including New York, had been taken from the Dutch in the year of London's great fire. The Dutch settlers found that they had more freedom under the new flag than before. They were soon joined by all kinds of people who were escaping from religious troubles; Englishmen, Scots, Swedes, Germans and Frenchmen. Most were Protestant, but English Catholics came too. Here was complete religious and political freedom.

The New England colonies in the north were rather different. Their people were extreme Protestants from southern England, and they refused to give others the freedom that they claimed for themselves. They regarded their Church as their government. Only strong royal pressure had forced them to give political rights to members of other Churches. But they were hard-working people, and their port of Boston attracted ships from all the world.

There were other differences too. The settled coastal people traded with Europe and kept in touch with foreign politics. Their brothers inland neither knew nor cared what happened in the old world that they had left behind them. Their faces were set towards the west, towards the wide open spaces, where a man might start a new life and forget the unhappy past. They wanted freedom from all government, whether royal or colonial.

The only thing that united them all was independence of spirit. This was soon shown when George III tried to tax them. The war against French Canada had cost a lot of money, and it still seemed necessary to keep a small defence force in the colonies. It was reasonable to expect the colonists to help with the costs, but the matter should have been referred to their councils. Instead of doing so, the King persuaded parliament to tax their imports of tea. The result was the famous 'Boston tea-party', when angry colonists emptied a ship-load of tea into the harbour.

The King's revenge was unwise and severe. First he closed the port of Boston. Then he ordered that the tea-party men should be sent to London for trial. All thirteen colonies rose in Boston's support. For the first time in their history they held a joint council, called the United States Congress, which declared their complete independence of Britain.

It was a declaration of war, but even now war could have been prevented by calm discussion. Unfortunately the weak Prime Minister, Lord North, let his cabinet be influenced by the King against parliament's advice. Public opinion was divided. Most people at first supported the government out of habit; but they were unwilling to join the army for such a cause. The King had to send professional .German soldiers, which made the colonists angrier than ever.

The colonists had a great leader in George Washington. He was born in Virginia, where his English grandparents had settled. He had already fought against the French. He was a good organizer and knew how to bring discipline and unity to his forces. From the start, he had one clear aim: to turn the thirteen colonies into a free American nation.

Washington had difficulty in persuading Congress to do what he wanted, but many mistakes were made by the British generals and politicians. There was no Chatham in the cabinet to take command. Indeed, the three most powerful voices in parliament were raised against the war; they were the voices of Chatham, Burke and Fox.

The French King now saw the opportunity of winning back Canada, and he joined the war on the American side. He soon regretted this; his men carried back to France a new spirit of freedom which destroyed him and his feudal society completely.

Spain, too, seized the chance of revenge on her old enemy: she attacked Gibraltar for three years without success. Forty years later, Britain in her turn took her revenge by helping the Spanish American colonies to win their independence.

George Washington's victory at Yorktown in 1781 gave new strength to the cabinet's enemies in parliament. Chatham was dead, but his younger son was attacking the war as 'the devil's work'. The House of Commons stated 'that the influence of the crown is increasing and .must be reduced'. Then it passed a formal declaration that the war must be stopped. Lord North resigned and the royal power was broken. Since that day, the cabinet has been responsible first to parliament, and only secondly to the King.

It was the end of a war that the British people had never wanted. Sooner or later the American colonies had to be free; otherwise they could not have become the great nation that they are today. But it was sad that their freedom had to be won by war with their own flesh and blood.

When Pitt became Prime Minister at the age of twenty-four, he was determined not to repeat the mistakes that had lost America. There were only a few years before France disturbed the peace of Europe. During that time, his treatment of colonial affairs did much to repair the damage that Britain's reputation had suffered. The shores of Australia had recently been explored by Captain James Cook, who had guided Wolfe's ships to Quebec. Pitt now organized the first settlements on the east Australian coast. He also worked out new systems of government for India and Canada, which allowed them to develop in peace during Napoleon's wars. Only the outbreak of these wars delayed his plans to end the slave trade.

In ancient times slaves were a normal prize of war. The practice died out in Europe before the Renaissance, but in Africa it spread. There, slaves were both the cause and the result of war. Tribe attacked tribe in order to seize human beings and sell them to traders for the Arab slave-market.

When European traders first visited West Africa they were offered slaves in exchange for their goods. Many refused to take them. Others agreed only because there was a heavy demand for workers in America. For the next two hundred years slaves were carried to Spanish America, the West Indies and the cotton-growing states. The voyage was cruel and so were some employers. Others treated them no worse than serfs on a feudal manor.

Most people in Britain knew little about this far-off trade until they heard Lord Mansfield's famous judgment: that any slave who set foot in Britain became a free man. Then a society was formed to stop it, but their efforts were resisted by the industrial north, which depended on cheap supplies of American cotton.

The American war gave the society new hope; their ideas were supported in parliament by men like Burke, Fox and Wilberforce.

In 1807 the trade was stopped, and in due course parliament bought the freedom of all slaves in the West Indies for £20 million. The American slaves were freed in 1865 when President Lincoln won his war against the southern states. But in Africa the tribes still fought each other and sold their slaves to the Arab market as they had always done. There would be no end to it until British influence spread inland from the coast.

*The Battle of Quatre Bras in 1815,
during the Napoleonic Wars*

A material factory in 1835

20

The War against Napoleon

Lord Nelson

William Pitt's first Tory government lasted for seventeen years, in which the King, George III, suffered from long fits of madness. This was awkward for a prime minister, but it gave him the chance to settle the future pattern of cabinet rule without royal interference.

Though he led the Tory party, he held more advanced views on social problems than almost anybody in parliament. At the age of fourteen he had entered Cambridge University, where he was deeply influenced by Adam Smith's *Wealth of Nations*. His strong feelings on such matters as slavery and colonial freedom were shared by Whig rivals like Fox and Burke, but there the likeness ended. His rivals were powerful critics whose fine talk had less effect when they were in office. Pitt himself was essentially practical and completely honest. He understood the relation of politics to commerce and he saw clearly the changes that industrial development made necessary.

The American war had left Britain heavily in debt. Pitt's tax reforms quickly improved trade and public confidence, but his plans for reform of parliament were resisted until it was too late. The terrible events in France in 1789 frightened parliament so badly that all talk of reform became unlawful. Europe was soon fighting for its life against the power of Napoleon; so Pitt was forced by the hard rules of war to prevent the social progress which at heart he wanted.

Most of Britain at first welcomed the ideas of the Paris reformers, who seemed likely to destroy the French feudal outlook and to improve foreign relations. She took no part in the vain attempt of Germany and Austria to save the French King. The killing of many members of the French upper classes disgusted her, but it was not her business to interfere. But then the French army seized Holland and Belgium. This was serious trouble, for the freedom of these two countries was essential to the balance of power. A foreign army in Belgium was a threat to the English shores.

In spite of this threat, Pitt was unwilling to make a direct attack. For the next fifteen years, his navy fought the French at sea while the powers of central Europe fought them on land. By attacking their colonies and their ships he aimed to stop all supplies from reaching them.

The war on land at first went badly. Then Admiral Nelson gave Europe fresh courage by destroying a French naval force at the mouth of the River Nile. The Mediterranean came under his control, with bases at Malta and Gibraltar, but France still had enough ships to threaten the Channel. At last, in 1805, he destroyed the rest of the enemy navy in the Battle of Trafalgar.

Nelson was killed in the hour of victory, but he is remembered as one of the best-loved commanders in the island's long history. Marlborough's success had been popular, but he himself was never liked. Wellington, the 'Iron Duke', was respected and feared. But Nelson knew and loved the men who served him.

He had joined the navy at the age of twelve, when his natural sympathy helped him to understand the problems of all ranks. His father was a parish priest without money or influence, so he had to make his way by his own efforts, but these efforts brought him to the personal notice of Pitt, who gave him his first important command. Today Nelson stands high above Trafalgar Square in the heart of London, and navy leaders gather there each year to do him honour on Trafalgar Day.

Pitt died a few months after his great admiral, and the war took a new turn. Napoleon attacked Spain and Portugal, and Britain was bound by treaty to go to help Portugal. The Duke of Wellington was sent with an army which fought the enemy in Spain while the rest of Europe struggled for its freedom. At first the central powers were defeated for lack of popular support; the anger of their people was not stirred until they began to suffer under French rule. Napoleon's ambition was to conquer the world, and he would let nothing stand in his way. He even seized Rome and imprisoned the Pope.

Meanwhile he was fighting a trade battle with Britain. His ports were forbidden to export anything to the island, and the British navy in return would not allow any ship to enter them. This led to trouble with the Americans. Merchant companies on each side of the ocean did their best to arrange a settlement, but both governments were deaf to reason. At the last moment the cabinet agreed to free American trade, but it was too late. Before the news reached the U.S. government, they took Napoleon's side and declared war on Britain. Their attacks on British ships did not change the course of the war, but their relations with Canada were severely damaged.

In 1812, Napoleon attacked Russia, but his forces were driven back from Moscow with heavy losses. His enemies took fresh courage. Wellington's army entered France from the south while the forces of Russia, Prussia, Austria and Sweden attacked across the Rhine. Napoleon was defeated and taken to the island of Elba, off the Italian coast. His escape next year, 1815, led to one more battle, when the allies under Wellington defeated him at Waterloo.

Other countries sent their kings to discuss conditions of peace, but George III was now completely mad. Britain was represented by Wellington and Lord Castlereagh, the Foreign Minister. The good sense of Castlereagh and the Russian King prevented any revenge being taken on France, so that western Europe now had many years of peace. Britain gave back most enemy colonies, but she kept a few that she needed to protect her trade. Of these, Malta and Mauritius and the Seychelles Islands had belonged to France; Ceylon and Singapore and Cape Town had belonged to Holland, which had fought on the French side.

Britain had fought France regularly from Hastings to Waterloo, for nearly 750 years. But since the peace treaty of 1815 the two countries have been friends.

The war against Napoleon came at a most unfortunate time in Britain's history. Her industrial development demanded widespread political and social changes which were impossible in time of war. Strikes and trade unions were made unlawful, though the best employers favoured unions. The government was too busy to keep in touch with the movement of population to the north. New towns grew up around the factories and mills; but they had no proper water-supply, no churches or schools or hospitals.

Who would listen to their complaints? They had no local government, no court and no representative in parliament. Even a town like Manchester had no member in the Commons, though the little county of Cornwall had forty-four.

Britain already depended on imported corn to feed her growing population. When the war prevented import from Europe, prices rose; but the government's remedy was unwise. Instead of controlling the price of corn or raising wages, they paid an allowance to every poor worker. This was harmful to the worker's self-respect. It also increased taxes. New forms of tax included Income Tax, which is paid on all earnings, and Death Duty, which is paid on a man's wealth when he dies.

As the war went on, the unity of the nation was broken by a strange new spirit of ill-feeling between town and country, between farm and factory. In the towns there was also a new class-feeling between employers and workers; the new type of manufacturer was an ambitious businessman whose only interest was in his profits. He did not care how his workers lived in the cheap rows of ill-built houses that he put up round his factory. The rich became richer. The middle class lived on their luck but were often ruined, liked Mr. Sedley in Thackeray's *Vanity Fair*. The poor suffered. Conditions were made worse by the flow of poor workers from Ireland, which had just been united with Britain. But the worst effect of all was the change in family life. Women no longer had their cottage industry; they went to work in the factories and took their children with them.

The capital still had a steadying influence on other towns. Its rapidly increasing population was composed mostly of office clerks, skilled workers in special trades, and rough workers in the port. But it was growing fast, and the old walled city was now only a small part of Greater London, which was spreading south across the river and west to Hyde Park and Paddington.

*An election scene from Dickens's
'Pickwick Papers'*

Victorian Birmingham

2 1

An early letter box

The Victorians in Politics and Industry

The defeat of Napoleon allowed the government to turn at last to home affairs. But the cost of the war left it without money, just when money was badly needed for social services. There were many unemployed, for scientific agriculture had reduced the demand for farm-workers before industry was ready to take them over. Many went overseas, the Scots to Canada and the English to Australia. They were not looking for trade or religious freedom; they were driven by the pressure of increasing population to find empty lands where they could settle and farm.

When the war stopped, corn prices should have gone down: but the corn laws kept the price up to encourage production at home. The government was more interested in developing trade than in social and political reform. Reduced customs-duties encouraged West Indian sugar, Canadian wood and Australian wool. Gradually trade improved and unemployment decreased, until at last it was possible to make strikes and trade unions lawful again.

For the next fifty years British industrial development raced far ahead of that of any other country. How did this happen? The answer lies chiefly in the bold use of capital. The upper classes took a close interest in science and discovery; they were willing to risk their money on mechanical inventions and new methods of production. The middle classes followed their example and put their savings into industrial shares; and the whole system was controlled by experienced commercial bankers. Meanwhile the navy protected the ships which brought raw materials and returned with manufactured goods to the busy markets of the world.

The biggest trade was in cotton goods, and the import of raw American cotton rose from eight thousand tons in 1760 to three hundred thousand tons in 1860. But heavier industry was beginning to take its place. New engineering works rose beside the coalfields of Cardiff and Birmingham, Sheffield and Newcastle and Glasgow.

In 1818 the first steamship crossed the Atlantic, and seven years later the first railway was opened to the public. George Stephenson, the inventor of the railway engine, was a fine example of the new class of mechanical worker, for he had no education. He taught himself to read at the age of seventeen. To encourage clever boys like him, special evening classes for mechanical workers were opened all over the country.

Cheap carriage and efficient business organization were essential to the new trade. Before the first steamer went to sea, a network of shipping lines already covered the world with two and a half million tons under sail. A network of railways soon covered Britain, and light-houses reduced the danger of shipwreck on the island's rocky coasts.

The world's first proper postal system kept manufacturers, shippers and buyers in close touch. A postmaster-general had been appointed by Queen Anne to run the old mail-coach service, but it was very expensive. In 1840 the penny post at last made it possible for even the poor to keep in touch with their absent families. The use of postage stamps was soon copied abroad, but the world still recognizes Britain's right to print stamps without her name on them.

For urgent affairs men could use the electric telegraph which ran beside the railway lines. The mad rush of modern commerce was already disturbing the sleepy offices of London, where every bright young clerk was using Pitman's new shorthand writing.

Meanwhile both social and political reforms were taking place. The Tory party's sixty years in office ended in 1830. They had led the country to victory over Napoleon and given it great industrial power, but on matters of reform they were divided. The reformers were grouped around Canning, the Foreign Minister, but they were outnumbered by the opposite group under Wellington.

This fierce old Duke was the only soldier who ever became Prime Minister of Britain, and even he could see the need for changes. Catholics and members of the Free Church were still forbidden to take public office, and Catholics could not sit in parliament. This was especially annoying to the Irish since their union with Britain in 1801; they were mostly Catholic but their representatives had to be Protestants. King George IV had refused to end these religious bars, but Wellington forced him to agree.

It was the last act of the great Tory age. For the next hundred years the two parties followed each other in and out of power. Before long they changed their names from Tory and Whig to Conservative and Liberal, but they both won their elections on promises of reform. The Conservatives attacked the evils of the towns, which mostly voted Liberal; and their rivals attacked the evils of the country, which mostly voted Conservative. From this healthy rivalry modern British society gradually developed.

The death of George IV caused an election which brought the Liberals to power with a strong programme of parliamentary reform. Strange to say, the cabinet that carried out these reforms was composed mostly of lords. The Prime Minister was Lord Grey, and his fellows included three future prime ministers: Lords Russell, Melbourne and Palmerston.

In 1832 their first reform bill took away one hundred and forty-three seats from empty country places and gave them to towns, for even Birmingham and Manchester still had no representative. The House of Lords voted against it, but they changed their minds when King William IV threatened to make enough new Liberal lords to pass it. This was a victory for cabinet rule. It was also proof that the reserve powers of a king could still be used to support the will of his people.

Two years later the Houses of Parliament were destroyed by fire. It was accidental, but it came at a good moment. The new buildings are a splendid exception to Victorian bad taste. In the clock tower the great bell, Big Ben, strikes the hour for radio listeners all over the world.

The Conservative party learnt a useful lesson from Lord Grey's success. Their next government was led by Sir Robert Peel, who formed the first regular police force. Every policeman was known as a 'Bobby', which is the friendly form of the name Robert. It was a suitable name, for the British police have always been the friends of the people. They have never been armed with anything but a short stick, and they rarely use even that.

Peel stopped the customs-duty on foreign corn and began a system of free trade which rapidly developed the commerce of Britain and the colonies. He also stopped the use of women and children in the coal-mines, and improved their conditions in the factories.

Such laws were strongly supported by good employers like Robert Owen. Owen was a Manchester mill-owner who developed a model factory. His system showed that attention to health and education could improve his employees' work as well as their standards of living.

He also tried to start a 'grand national trade union', but the workers were not ready for such a bold advance. They were certainly not interested in such a trouble-maker as the German Jew, Karl Marx. When Marx was driven out of Europe he settled in London to write his books, which called for class war and the end of private property. But British trade unions were content to improve the wages and conditions of workers by lawful and reasonable means.

On Peel's death Benjamin Disraeli became the leader of the Conservative party, and he persuaded it to give the vote to all industrial workers. For the rest of the century the two parties were competing for popularity. Gladstone's Liberals reformed the army and the school system. He gave the public service new standards of honest efficiency; in future a strict check of public accounts would prevent all bribery and improper influence. He also arranged for secret voting at elections. Disraeli followed with improvements to public health and housing. Gladstone returned and gave the vote to agricultural workers. But then he made a great mistake.

In the election of 1885 the parties were so evenly balanced that neither could form a government without the help of the Irish Catholic party. Gladstone accepted their help, and he promised them self-government in exchange.

The British public was extremely angry, for Gladstone's election programme had not provided for such action. It would have been less serious if he had only offered his Irish friends the control of the Catholic south, but he offered them Ulster too. Protestant Ulster was more than angry, it was ready to fight for its right to remain united with Britain. Gladstone's own party turned against him, and he was forced to resign.

For most of the next twenty years the Conservatives governed under Lord Salisbury, a descendant of Queen Elizabeth's chief minister, Cecil. By now elected councils had been set up for all levels of local government: the county, the town, the country district and the parish. Their members were all independent, for the British people were suspicious of party interference in their local affairs. In recent years party politics have taken control of councils in London and most big towns; but country people still prefer to elect independent members.

Countrymen had good reason to distrust all politicians, for their interests had been shamefully neglected by both parties. When the customs-duty was taken off imported corn, Disraeli warned parliament that cheap foreign corn would destroy British agriculture. Nobody listened to him, and at first the change seemed to have no effect.

Although most farmland belonged to the big landowners, the farms themselves were usually rented by squires and yeomen. Half the farms in the land were still family affairs. Landlords built good brick cottages for their workers, at low rents. Enclosure was stopped so that common land could be kept for public enjoyment; the value of fresh air and exercise for indoor workers was at last being recognised.

For thirty years Disraeli's warnings were forgotten. Then suddenly he was proved right, and the products of Britain's industry began to destroy her agriculture. Cheap corn from the wide open spaces of America flooded in and ruined the home farmers. Why was it so cheap? Because British machinery made mass production possible. Because it was carried from farm to market by trains and ships that were made of British iron and steel.

British farmers turned from corn to sheep and cattle, as they had after the Black Death. But soon this trade began to feel the competition of frozen meat from Australia and New Zealand. There too, the wide open spaces allowed large-scale farming which a thickly populated island could not copy.

So long as cheap food came from abroad to feed the town workers, neither Liberals nor Conservatives seemed to care what happened to the farmers. There was no unemployment problem, as industry could use all those who moved out of the country into the towns. Britain's agriculture was left to decay until the First World War, when foreign food stopped coming and her people were left hungry.

Queen Victoria and the royal family

A school in Bristol in 1895

22

The Victorians at Home and Abroad

A Victorian silver ornament

When parliament in 1867 gave the vote to all industrial workers, it suddenly realized that most of them could not read. 'If we are the servants of the people,' members said, 'we must educate our masters.'

The problem of education was so closely connected with religion that no government had ever dared to act on it. Britain had suffered too much from religious quarrels in the past, and strong feelings still lay close beneath the surface of parliamentary life. But Gladstone now became Prime Minister, and he was one of those severe Victorians whose sense of moral duty outweighed all fears.

The various Churches did their best to supply simple education for the masses, but they could not keep up with the growing popular demand. Their country schools were often supported by generous squires, but in the new towns it was difficult to find the necessary money. Largely as a result of better health services, the population of eleven million in 1800 had risen to thirty-one million by 1870. At least half was in the towns.

Anglicans favoured a system of state schools under the control of the state Church. Others thought that the State should take over all church schools. Gladstone disagreed with both these views. He decided to open state schools wherever they were needed, without any religious control; but he also provided money to help the Churches to build more schools of their own. Within a few years, all parents were forced by law to send their children to school. Employers were also forbidden to give them full-time jobs till they were fourteen.

The government's plans were supported by public opinion for unexpected reasons. Prussia, the most powerful German state, had just defeated France in war, and her success was believed to be the result of high standards of education. No doubt it was true, for each future war proved the need for better schools; the Education Acts of 1902, 1918 and 1944 were the results. Gradually the State extended its influence over the church schools. By sharing their costs it gained a share in their control, until most of them came entirely into its hands. But even today there are one and a half million children in church schools.

The universities also profited from Gladstone's reforms. Oxford and Cambridge were at last allowed to admit students who did not belong to the Anglican Church, and their College Fellows were at last allowed to marry. Before the end of the century they were admitting women students and encouraging more scientific studies; in this they were following the example of the new University of London.

Industrial wealth brought a large increase in the middle classes, who knew the value of good education and were willing to pay for it. Their demands produced many new independent schools. Some of these were local private schools: others were public schools like Wellington and Marlborough, which quickly earned a high reputation. Most public schools had always been more interested in teaching Latin than in training boys to become useful citizens. But the Victorian conscience now provided a new sort of headmaster, and the greatest of them was Thomas Arnold of Rugby.

Rugby school was opened in Elizabethan days and is best known as the home of Rugby football. This new game was just becoming popular when Arnold was made headmaster in 1828. He regarded organized games as a means of teaching fair play and sportsmanship. His ideas of discipline were based on trust instead of force, and he gave the oldest boys official responsibilities. He believed that a school's most important duty was character-training. It should teach boys to give honest service and responsible leadership, whatever their future employment might be. One of his pupils, Thomas Hughes, has shown us in *Tom Brown's Schooldays* something of Arnold's influence on the school.

But his influence stretched wider than that, not only into other schools but across the world. In the past all officials of the public service, at home or overseas, had been appointed by personal recommendation only. When Gladstone opened this profession to all, by a system of written examination, it was filled largely by young men who had been brought up according to Arnold's educational ideas.

Queen Victoria and her German husband, Prince Albert, took a keen interest in education as well as in art, religion and foreign affairs. They also set an example of happy family life. They liked to travel and they built a royal castle at Balmoral, where they could learn something of Scottish life and meet their highland people.

Then Albert died, and the Queen was rarely seen in public again, though she lived for another forty years. Unhappiness turned her into a cold and severe old woman. History too easily forgets the girl who became Queen at eighteen, and remembers only the solemn widow of Windsor.

English people today tend to laugh at the strict morality of the Victorian age, and it is true that many Victorians were too self-satisfied. Like Cromwell's supporters, many regarded pleasure as sin, and poverty as God's punishment for laziness. Daily family prayers and Sunday Bible-reading reminded their children that obedience was the greatest virtue.

They believed every word of the Bible, so that Darwin's scientific ideas about the origin of man raised a loud public outcry. The battle between faith and reason had begun in earnest. Bishops angrily resisted the suggestion that they were descended from monkeys; the scientists replied that they would rather be descended from monkeys than from bishops. Yet Darwin was a good Christian, and he believed that a scientific study of God's world could lead to better understanding of God's purpose and man's duty.

The early Victorian father would not even discuss matters of which he disapproved. He had fixed ideas, especially about women. A woman's place was in the home; she had no right to look for interesting employment outside it. Even in the home, her interests and conversation were strictly controlled.

But no disapproval could silence Florence Nightingale, whose courage saved the lives of thousands of soldiers in the Crimean War of 1855. This war was a local effort by France and Britain to keep Russian influence out of the eastern Mediterranean. It came at a time when newspapers had begun to guide public opinion. Newspaper men went with the army to the Crimea, and the war reporter of *The Times* was severely critical of the inefficient army hospitals. He was supported by the newly-born *Daily Telegraph*, the first penny newspaper.

At that time there was no nursing profession; men died of their wounds in dirty army hospitals when a little care and cleanliness would have saved them. Florence had friends in high places, and she persuaded them to let her take charge of the base hospital near Istanbul. The 'Lady with the Lamp' (as the soldiers called her) and her group of nurses were so successful that her ideas quickly spread at home.

The nursing profession gave women their first chance to prove their independence. Many large schools for girls were already being run by private and religious bodies, and soon the universities were open to them. The invention of the bicycle helped the young lady to escape from mother's watchful eye and from the uncomfortable clothing of polite society. Skirts became shorter, and girls could even play ball-games like tennis and hockey.

The Victorians enjoyed the fine arts. They liked to read poetry and stories, to look at pictures and to listen to music. But they had little taste in building and furniture. They built ugly rows of un-healthy little houses for their town workers, and large ugly houses for themselves. Their furniture was heavy and they took especial delight in useless ornament. Electricity was coming into use in city centres. Most of London had been lit by gas since the end of Napoleon's wars, and its use had spread to other towns. But country people and the industrial poor still had to use oil.

The social customs, politics and popular feelings of Britain can be followed in the drawings and articles of *Punch*, a magazine which has appeared weekly since 1841. Its jokes of a hundred years ago can still make us laugh, but many of them had a critical purpose. Not only the Churches had a social conscience; some writers of early Victorian days had a powerful effect on social reform.

Charles Dickens did as much as any man to draw his country's attention to the needs of the poor. He was especially sorry for children who had no parents, or whose parents were in prison, for his own father had been in prison for debt. The characters of history and of most literature belong to the middle and upper classes of society, but Dickens writes of the poor and the humble. His first book took his middle-class Mr. Pickwick to prison and showed him the terrible conditions inside.

It was followed by sad but exciting stories of poor and fatherless children: *Oliver Twist*, *The Old Curiosity Shop*, *David Copperfield*, *Great Expectations* and many more. Such books had a great influence on those who pressed parliament to improve conditions in factories and prisons, and to care for homeless children.

The best-known memorial in London is the figure of Eros, the Greek god of love, in Piccadilly Circus. It stands in memory of the seventh Lord Shaftesbury, who spent his life pushing social reforms through parliament. One of his laws stopped the use of little boys as chimney-sweepers, but it might not have been passed without the help of Kingsley's *Water Babies*. This book described how boys were forced to climb up inside dark and dangerous chimneys because men were too lazy to use a long brush. It set a new fashion in books that were written especially for children.

The nineteenth century produced great poetry too, but three of the greatest poets died young before Victoria became Queen: Byron in Greece, Keats and Shelley in Italy. All three were lovers of Greek and Roman art and thought; they aimed to express the ancient ideals of beauty in their own fresh English verse. Wordsworth shared their ideals and opened his countrymen's eyes to the beauties of nature. But the true representative of the Victorian age was Tennyson. He was a patriotic poet who wrote with equal pride of King Arthur's knights and of modern cavalry charges. He was a dreamer too, who looked ahead to the 'parliament of man' that should put an end to war.

Wordsworth's poetry attracted his readers to visit the Lake District where he lived, for the holiday habit was taking hold of the British people. Many factory workers, especially in the north, began to take their families to the seaside; the middle class went to the Lakes, to Cornwall, or to the Welsh and Scottish mountains; the upper class developed a fashionable colony on the south coast of France, which was then quiet and unspoilt.

But travel abroad was no longer reserved for the rich. Thomas Cook, the travel-agent, was beginning to arrange tours to France,

Italy, Austria and Switzerland. British climbers explored the Alps. An English artist, Edward Whymper, was the first man to climb the Matterhorn. This success excited much interest, and mountain-climbing became a sport which ninety years later took a British party to conquer Everest, the world's highest point.

The greatest travellers of all were those who set out to explore the unknown places of the world, especially in Africa. There were also some who distinguished themselves by taking part in foreign wars. The poet Byron fought and died in the Greek struggle for freedom from Turkish rule. When Spanish America broke away from Spain, a party of British officers served on Simón Bolivar's staff; meanwhile Chile's navy was led by Admiral Cochrane, the member of parliament for Westminster.

The British government sympathized with such causes. Its influence also helped Garibaldi to unite the many states of Italy into one strong country. It still aimed to strengthen the balance of power in Europe, and the Foreign Minister, Lord Palmerston, played a leading part in helping Belgium to gain her independence. Palmerston's influence guided foreign affairs for fifty years after Waterloo, and he arranged a treaty in which the Great Powers promised to respect Belgium's independence. Seventy-five years later, this treaty brought Britain into the First World War.

Part of the Canadian Pacific railway in 1877

A nineteenth-century Australian sheep farm

23

The Victorian Empire

England's first colonists were the merchant explorers of Elizabethan days, who went in search of new lands for trade. They were followed by those who wanted freedom from the religious troubles of the seventeenth century; these too were mostly supported by merchants at home. They did not have to fight for their lands; the existing population was so small and unsettled that there was room for all.

Bermuda was settled in 1609. The various islands of the West Indies were either settled directly or taken from the French and Spaniards. Jamaica, the largest, was taken from Spain in 1655. Most islands imported African slaves to work their farms, but the social position of these workers improved after parliament had bought their freedom. They could have gone back to Africa, where the colony of Sierra Leone offered them a special welcome. But most preferred to stay, and in due course their descendants became rulers of the islands.

Eighteenth-century settlers were mostly Scots from the newly-opened highlands, but the growth of the Victorian empire was on a far greater scale. In the sixty years after Waterloo nearly eight million people left Britain, and half of them went to the United States. The successful settlement of the other half was largely due to two men, Gibbon Wakefield and Lord Durham. Wakefield's book, *The Art of Colonisation*, was widely read. He also formed the New Zealand Association and the South Australia Association, which organized settlement of those lands in an orderly manner.

The Churches helped too. Elsewhere the British government has had to resist the Churches' desire to press Christianity on every kind of people. Its official views have always given equal respect and equal rights to Muslims, Hindus, Buddhists and Christians. It has welcomed the Churches' help with schools and hospitals, but it has not allowed them to interfere with other faiths. In Australia and New Zealand there was no such problem and the Churches were free to use all their power, with excellent results.

Durham was a cabinet minister who became Governor-General of Canada in 1837. Under Wakefield's influence he realized that self-government would not separate the colonies, it would bind them closer to the mother country. When he reached Canada he found that English-speaking Ontario and French-speaking Quebec were sharply divided; they disliked each other and they disliked their British governors even more. Durham united them as one self-governing colony. They were already united in resistance to the U.S.A., which had attacked them during Napoleon's wars.

The border was now fixed in a straight line from the Great Lakes to the Pacific Ocean. On both sides of it, bold explorers gradually made their way further west and started new colonies. In 1867 the east Canadian colonies became an independent dominion, and later they were joined by others until all Canada became one land from coast to coast. Meanwhile the Canadian Pacific Railway gave practical effect to their political unity.

A self-governing colony leaves defence and foreign affairs to the mother country. A dominion is a completely free nation that owes loyalty to the crown alone. In Canada each former colony kept its own parliament to control local affairs, so that Quebec still has its old French flavour. French and English are joint official languages, and the dominion parliament meets in the capital at Ottawa.

Australia's first colonies were prison settlements. For a long time, British courts had punished criminals by sending them to the American colonies. In fact many of them were not really criminals; a man could be sent for the smallest offence. When the Americans became independent, a new prison settlement at Sydney became the first colony in Australia. Ordinary settlers soon followed and began to raise sheep and cattle. Freed prisoners chose to remain as farmers, so did their guards on retirement. Settlements all round the coast

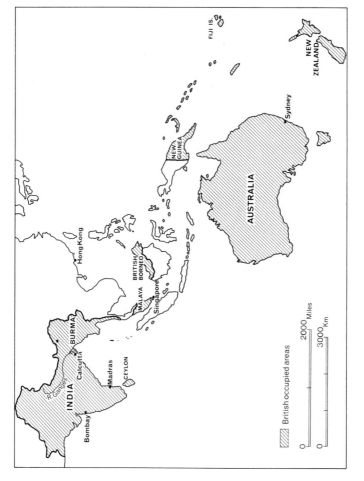

The Empire in the East in 1939

British occupied areas

2000 Miles
3000 Km

developed into self-governing colonies, as in Durham's Canada. Gradually the railways joined them together, until in 1901 they were united in one dominion.

Australia had no race problems, and she was determined not to make any by admitting workers from Asian lands. Her people formed a classless society which was prepared to work hard for its living. The land was large, and much of it was desert. But hard work and imaginative government have turned it into a busy modern state which helps to feed and clothe the world; for it has twenty million cattle and eight times that number of sheep.

New Zealand is a small country which is so like Britain that colonists quickly felt at home there. Her coasts were first explored by Captain Cook; but organized settlement was begun by Wakefield's association and the Churches sixty years later. She was soon given self-government, with equal rights for her small Maori population, and in 1907 she became a dominion. Like Australia, she raises an immense number of sheep and cattle.

British settlers in Canada, Australia and New Zealand were true colonists who went to make new homes in empty lands. Nearly all of them were countrymen who knew well how to look after themselves. In their native villages in Britain they had grown their own food, built their own houses, made their own clothes and furniture. They settled down to farm their new lands in peace, as no man's rival.

British settlements in India and Africa were of a different kind. The charter companies sent men to trade, not to make homes, and the usual pattern of events was as follows. The traders were welcomed by the coastal peoples, they set up trading stations, and they made friendly agreements with local rulers. But sooner or later they and their hosts were attacked by jealous inland peoples. To protect themselves, they employed armed forces of local men under British officers.

Meanwhile other European powers were doing the same thing; the French in India, the French and Germans in Africa, the French and Dutch in Asia. Competition for the friendship of local rulers grew fiercer as the nineteenth century passed. Other powers took official possession of lands where they traded, but the British government was unwilling to do so. It tried to work through the charter companies, till the last possible moment.

French rivalry led to the gradual extension of British control over the whole of India, which had been left in confusion by the breakdown of the Mogul Empire. This control remained in the hands of the East India Company, but it was under a governor-general who was responsible to the prime minister. At first the company's staff had been entirely British, but in 1833 it was laid down that 'no native of India shall be prevented from holding any office or employment because of his religion, descent or colour'. English was taken as the official language of education, which opened to Indians the literature and the universities of Europe. The company began to develop railways, roads, schools, hospitals and water-supplies; in fact it was providing social services which were not yet universal in Britain herself. But the extreme poverty and the deep-rooted customs of India's ever-increasing population made social progress as slow and difficult as it still is today.

The peace of India was broken in 1857 when soldiers in the upper Ganges districts rose against their officers. The rest of the country remained loyal, and Indian and British forces fought side by side to put down the rising. The British government then took over from the company as rulers of both India and Burma; but only half India was under direct rule, the other half was composed of self-governing states. Political development was a difficult problem, as it always is in a country where different races and religions must mix; moreover, India was as big as many European countries put together.

Meanwhile Ceylon and the Malay states were making peaceful progress under the British flag. So were Fiji and a mass of other Pacific islands, which were developing a useful trade with Australia and New Zealand. By now a chain of islands and ports protected the empire's trade. Gibraltar, Malta and Cyprus covered the passage from Britain to the Suez Canal, which was guarded in the south by Aden. St. Helena, where Napoleon died, lay on the way to Cape Town; and Mauritius lay between that and India. Beyond all these, the little-known islands of Singapore and Hong Kong were being turned into the greatest ports of all Asia.

Mengo Hill in Uganda

A look-out post during the Boer War

24

The Problems of Africa

Dr Livingstone

The story of Africa was very different. For three centuries the traders of western Europe —Portuguese, Dutch, Danes, French and British—had kept some small stations on the coast, but they had never managed to explore inland. Anyone who tried to do so was quickly killed by tribesmen or disease.

Then in the nineteenth century British explorers uncovered the secrets of Africa's rivers, the Nile, the Niger, the Congo and the Zambezi. They were independent men who travelled for the sake of discovery, often alone. Curiosity kept them going in spite of all dangers.

The fashion was set by a ship's doctor, Mungo Park, who reached Timbuktu from the west and explored the upper Niger. His *Travels in Africa* fired the imagination of his fellow countrymen. One of them, Captain Clapperton of the Royal Navy, crossed the Sahara Desert from the north and reached the ancient city of Kano; then he started again from the west and reached Kano once more. He died of fever, but his servant Lander completed his work by following the Niger down to the sea.

Most famous of them all was the Scottish doctor David Livingstone, who went out to work for a church society. He explored all across central Africa from coast to coast, and wherever he went he found slavery and disease.

Such discoveries were of little interest to the government, but they were of great interest to traders and the Churches. The traders wanted to make agreements with inland chiefs. The Churches wanted to spread their religion and stop slavery. On all Livingstone's travels he saw long lines of men and women, boys and girls, who were chained together and driven like cattle to the slave markets of the east coast. Britain had stopped the slave trade to America. Could she not stop it in the heart of Africa itself?

Public opinion demanded that the government should interfere. Only law and order could have any effect, but the government preferred to leave this to two new charter companies, the Royal Niger Company and the East Africa Company. Foreign threats to British trade at last persuaded the government to take over the Companies' responsibility at the turn of the century. The countries of Nigeria, Gold Coast (now Ghana), Kenya and Uganda were born, and slavery was stopped by law.

But the habit of centuries did not die easily, as one chief explained to his new governor: 'Can you stop a cat from catching mice? I shall die with a slave in my mouth!'

Meanwhile the Suez Canal had been a special problem. For centuries this corner of Africa had been part of the Turkish Empire. In 1875 the British government bought a controlling share in the Canal, which the French had built to provide a short sea passage to the east. Since Britain owned four-fifths of the world's steamships she had a natural interest in the Canal's safety. So when Turkish rule broke down a few years later, she brought in her forces to protect the Canal.

There was also trouble in the Sudan, which had risen against its Egyptian masters. The Sudan was then the greatest slave market in Africa. For some years an Egyptian force under a British officer had been struggling to stop the terrible trade. This force was now surrounded in Khartoum and its leader, General Gordon, was killed; but his death was largely the fault of Gladstone, who had refused to send help in time.

The British public never forgave Gladstone, for Gordon was a religious man and a popular figure. Khartoum was at last won back by a cavalry charge in which young Winston Churchill took part, and it remained under British rule till 1956. In this year the Canal was taken over by Egypt, which had become an independent state after the First World War.

South Africa was another problem. When the British took Cape

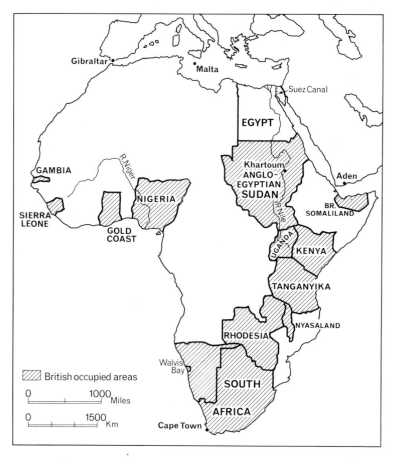

Gibraltar

Malta

Suez Canal

EGYPT

R.Niger

GAMBIA

Khartoum
ANGLO-
EGYPTIAN
SUDAN

Aden

NIGERIA

BR.
SOMALILAND

SIERRA
LEONE

GOLD
COAST

R.Nile

UGANDA

KENYA

TANGANYIKA

NYASALAND

RHODESIA

Walvis
Bay

British occupied areas

0   1000 Miles

0   1500 Km

SOUTH

AFRICA

Cape Town

The Empire in Africa in 1939

Town during Napoleon's wars, there was already a large population of Dutch farmers, called Boers. These people were happy enough until British colonists began to arrive in large numbers; then the Colonial Office laid down a policy of equal rights for all men, without regard to colour or race. The Boers disagreed. They moved north and began a new independent colony beyond the border. But British miners, traders and church workers followed them, and their troubles began again.

One of the most successful diamond miners was young Cecil Rhodes. He was ambitious. He wanted to unite the Dutch and British colonies, and he wanted to build a railway from Cape Town to Cairo. But first he had to prevent the Germans from seizing the land between their eastern and western colonies, in case they hindered his railway. He formed a new charter company to take over this land, which he called Rhodesia.

The sharply divided interests of Boer farmers and British miners led to war in 1899. After two years of struggle the Boers were defeated, but they taught the British army a valuable lesson. A soldier's red coat, for example, could be seen for miles; but the Boer in his rough brown clothes could creep up unseen, make a surprise attack, and disappear again among the rocks and bushes. Without the experience of this war, the British army would have been no match for the Germans in 1914.

Only one general could beat the Boers at their own tricks, and his name was Robert Baden-Powell. The ten million Boy Scouts in our modern world owe their existence to his experiences in this war, when he trained boy messengers to help his hard-pressed forces.

The defeated Boers were generously treated. Within a few years the Union of South Africa became a dominion, in which English and Dutch were joint official languages. In both World Wars the Boers fought on Britain's side. But they still outnumbered the population of British origin, and they still disagreed with the idea of race equality. When Britain began giving independence to her African colonies, the Union cut its last ties with the crown.

Perhaps the most famous writer about the Victorian empire was Rudyard Kipling. This poet and story-teller was born in India and grew up with a strong sense of the empire's purpose. He saw its value as a civilizing influence in the world and he wrote of Britain's responsibility to lead its peoples to a richer life.

He sympathized with the feelings of all who were concerned in the empire's development; its peoples of every race and religion, the soldiers who kept its peace, and the officials who ran its public services. But in each case his sympathy was drawn to the common man, not to the chiefs and generals and governors. His best-loved characters are humble people like Gunga Din, the water-carrier, or the homeless boy Kim. His powers of sympathetic observation so attracted Baden-Powell that he based the early training of his Boy Scouts on Kipling's stories of Indian boyhood.

Kipling's ideas of responsibility explain why parliament was unwilling to take over from the charter companies. A company is only expected to trade, but a colonial government is expected to provide every kind of social service. Countless millions of pounds would be needed to provide Africa with roads and railways, schools and hospitals. The profits of existing trade could not cover a thousandth of the cost. Who then was to pay? Certainly not the British taxpayer, who was still struggling to provide such services for his own people. Somehow the people of Africa would have to learn to pay their own way by producing goods for the export market. This would mean slow and gradual development, but it would be the best training for self-government.

British soldiers in France in the 1914–18 War

*Ration books to control each person's food
supply in the Second World War*

25

The Listener

The weekly magazine of BBC radio

The World at War

In the late nineteenth century Britain kept out of foreign politics as much as possible. Europe was divided into two camps: France and Russia in one, Germany, Austria and Italy in the other. Britain favoured the second group so long as France threatened her interests in Africa and the Russians threatened her Indian border. But Germany was growing too strong. The various German states had been united under the King of Prussia after his conquest of France in 1870. He was now Emperor of all Germany. He was Queen Victoria's son-in-law, but his ambitions took no account of such a tie. Britain watched him with growing mistrust.

The Germans already had the best army in Europe. By 1901, when Victoria died, they had begun to build a very large navy, which was not needed to protect their trade. It could only have one purpose, to fight its British rival. Edward VII had never shared his mother's faith in the Emperor's goodwill, and Britain now openly made friends with France. She would not make a defence treaty, but she showed that her sympathy would be with the French if the Germans attacked them. Plans were made for an army of 150,000 men which would be ready to cross the Channel at a moment's notice. When war came in 1914, this force managed to arrive just in time to save Paris.

Britain had no quarrel with Germany, and public opinion was divided on the question of supporting France. If the Germans had made a direct attack, they might have taken Paris before anyone interfered. But they attacked through Belgium. Their Emperor did not believe that Britain would go to war for 'a bit of paper', which was his scornful description of Palmerston's treaty. However, when he attacked Belgium, all Britain united against him, and half the nations of the world were soon fighting in the muddy ditches of France. Every part of the Empire immediately joined the British side, and three years later the United States followed their example. When the war was won, both sides had suffered immense losses. The Empire's forces had lost a million men, and Britain had spent all her wealth.

The war destroyed the power of the Liberal party, which had been in office for eight years when fighting started. During that time it had done much to tax the rich and to help the poor, especially the old and the workless. It had introduced insurance against illness and industrial accidents, and it had arranged regular medical examination of children. Local councils were given more power but less independence; they were helped by government money but they suffered from government interference.

The House of Lords did not like the ever-increasing taxes. In 1909 they refused to pass the budget, which is the government's yearly plan for getting and spending money. It included a Land Tax which the Prime Minister, Lloyd George, had put in on purpose, knowing that the majority of land-owning lords would resist it. It was a clever trap, and they fell straight into it. For centuries, custom had allowed them to refuse an ordinary bill; but this time they were refusing a budget because it was against their own interests. It was time that their power was reduced. The next year Edward VII died, and a new election showed that the people supported the government. Edward's son, now George V, had to make the Lords change their minds. He threatened to make new Liberal lords, just as William IV had done to pass Lord Grey's reform bill. The country was relieved to see that the royal power could still be used to support its will, and the position of the crown was strengthened.

The war had been won by a united Liberal–Conservative government under Lloyd George, but it was followed by an unwise peace treaty. The spirit of revenge ruled France, which had suffered most, and Lloyd George would not listen to his more moderate advisers.

The Americans quickly stopped taking any interest in the matter. An international parliament, called the League of Nations, was formed in Geneva; but America and Russia refused to join it. The severe treatment of Germany helped Hitler's rise to power, which the League was unable to stop.

The question of Irish independence was now settled at last. Protestant Ulster chose to remain in the United Kingdom. The rest of the island became a dominion until 1937, when it decided to leave the empire altogether and took the name of Eire. Eire kept out of the Second World War, but many of her men fought in the British forces.

Ulster has her own parliament in Belfast but she also sends twelve members to the House of Commons. The Isle of Man has its own parliament too, called the House of Keys. The Channel Islands are famous for their cattle, especially Jersey and Guernsey. They belonged to William the Conqueror and they still owe their loyalty to the crown, not to any government in London. Many of their people still speak old Norman French.

The Irish settlement split Lloyd George's government, and in 1924 the Labour party took office for the first time. But they tried to make friends with Communist Russia, and this was so unpopular that they were soon out of office. In 1929 they tried again. This time they lasted two years, but they had not the necessary experience to guide the country at a time when all the world was in trouble. A new election gave them only a tenth of parliament's seats.

The whole country was now so anxious to return to normal conditions that it took little notice of events in Europe. Only Winston Churchill had the courage to raise his voice in warning, and no one listened to him. The Americans still kept out of the League of Nations, which had no power to back up its views. Like everyone else, the British continued to believe Hitler's false promises of peace; Russia even made a treaty of friendship with him.

Hitler's broken promises included an attack on Poland, which Britain and France were bound by treaty to defend. But neither of them was armed in readiness for the Second World War, which began in September 1939. Within eight months France had fallen, and only Britain stood against Hitler's armies. The Empire supported her, but Russia and America still took no part in the struggle.

Then, in May 1940, Winston Churchill became Prime Minister of a government that combined all parties.

Later in the war, the army workshops had a saying: 'Difficult repairs are done at once; impossible repairs take a little longer'. Churchill had to make impossible repairs to his country's defences, and he made them at once. The British army of a quarter of a million men was rescued from the shores of Dunkirk (with a large part of the French army also) by hundreds of little boats that sailed from every harbour of the south and east. It had to leave its arms behind, and the German army waited eagerly for orders to cross the Channel and to seize the unarmed island.

But how could they cross while the Royal Navy still guarded the seas, and the Royal Air Force guarded the skies? Hitler did not dare to bring out his navy. Instead, he sent his air force to destroy Britain's southern airfields and then London. He failed. In three months he lost over 2,000 aeroplanes. This was the Battle of Britain. It was won by the skill and courage of those who flew a few hundred Spitfire and Hurricane fighters against Germany's thousands of more powerful machines. As Churchill said, 'Never . . . has so much been owed by so many to so few'.

But much was owed to Churchill himself. He formed a Home Guard. This was an army of citizens which would help to defend towns and villages if there was an enemy attack. Men and boys over seventeen armed themselves with any kind of weapon they could find. At the same time, Churchill's stirring speeches gave new hope and courage to the nation. They also influenced President Roosevelt of America, who was already planning to help Britain by sending arms.

'Hitler knows,' said Churchill, 'that he will have to break us in this island or lose the war. If we can stand up to him, all Europe may be free. But if we fail, then the whole world, including the United States, will sink into a new Dark Age.'

Churchill was already planning the future. His aims, as he had said, were not only to defend Britain but also to set Europe free. While the German army waited to cross the Channel, he sent Britain's only armoured division round the south of Africa to the Suez Canal. Its duty was to prepare the way for those armies which would one day attack Hitler's empire from the south. The next year Hitler attacked Russia, and Japan attacked America; this gave Churchill two strong allies to help him finish the struggle.

When the war was over, Britain had to turn her attention to problems inside the Empire. Many of the peoples who had helped to win the war, now demanded their independence. Britain accepted their right to make this demand. She was already planning to turn the Empire into a commonwealth of free and equal members. The word *commonwealth* explains itself, for its members are united for their common profit.

Religious problems caused India's division into two new independent states, India and Pakistan, in 1947. The next year Ceylon also became independent. Other countries needed an urgent development programme to improve education, commercial production and public services before they were ready to stand on their own feet. With the British tax-payer's help, this programme was carried out. Some of these countries would be stronger now if it had been carried out less hurriedly; but Britain was pressed by world opinion to hand over her responsibilities without delay. One by one, the former colonies became independent members of the British Commonwealth, and took their seats among the United Nations.

The pay desks at a modern food store, as seen through a mirror made by the Volomatic Company of Coventry

St. Paul's cathedral and the London skyline today

26

Crown and People in the Twentieth Century

A popular small car— the Mini

Victoria died in 1901 after sixty-four years as Queen. She had given the country a new idea of royalty. It was proud of her, as the head of a world-wide family of nations, but it also liked her simple tastes and orderly habits. Politically, her relations with the cabinet were correct and formal. She demanded to be kept informed of all that her government was doing. She discussed it with them. She objected to what she did not like. Often ministers accepted her advice, which was based on greater experience than theirs, but she left the decisions to them. It was fortunate for Britain that the growth of popular government was supported by closer understanding between crown and people.

Edward VII had been refused any share of royal duties by his mother while he was Prince of Wales. He now brought a new feeling of fashionable gaiety to public life. The Victorians had many good qualities, but they were inclined to be dull and serious. During the short Edwardian age, people could relax and begin to enjoy life more light-heartedly.

It also produced a new fighting spirit among the nation's women. They already had the right to vote in local elections and to be members of local government councils. Why, they asked, could they not have the same rights in respect of parliament? Their cause was widely supported in parliament itself, but it was not helped by the violence of a small group of women who fought the police, chained themselves to lamp-posts outside ministers' houses, and threw bricks through the windows. When the war came, women proved in the arms factories that they could do men's work; when it ended, they were given the vote and the right to enter parliament.

King George V set the new fashion that keeps the royal family in daily touch with the people—visiting schools and hospitals, farms and factories. His Jubilee Trust provided playing-fields for children, for he had seen the dirty and ugly back-streets which formed the only playground for London's cockney children. London now has more than eight million people, but it has no more cheerful citizens than the cockneys, who are the natives of London's east end: in the worst moments of the last war, when their homes were destroyed by nightly air attacks, they still managed to keep their sense of humour.

When George VI was a young man, he used to run boys' holiday camps. He himself had only two daughters, Elizabeth and Margaret. He was quiet by nature and he never expected to become King. But his elder brother, Edward VIII, wanted to marry an American woman who had already been married twice. Since she could not be Queen, Edward did not want to be King. In December 1936, before he had been crowned, he left the country and his brother George took his place. Then war came. In spite of the government's advice, George VI refused to leave London. His daily visits to the forces, the factories and the damaged towns cheered his people everywhere, but he always returned to Buckingham Palace, his London home.

Elizabeth II was visiting Kenya when she became Queen in 1952 on her father's death. Like her father and grandfather, she has travelled all over the world to meet her many peoples. She was brought up simply but carefully. Both she and her sister were Girl Guides, and during the war she received training in the women's branch of the army. Her marriage to Prince Philip of Greece in 1947 was extremely popular.

Philip is a descendant of Queen Victoria. He was brought up in Britain, and during the war he served with the Royal Navy. On his marriage he was given the title of Duke of Edinburgh. His great interest in science and industry, as well as in youth and sport, has fitted him to give the country a bold lead in matters outside politics.

Meanwhile, what was happening inside politics? The Labour party had become full-grown, and immediately after the war it had six years in office. It introduced a national health service, which had already been planned under Churchill's wartime government. It put the coal-mines and the railways under state control, and it aimed to extend this control to banking, insurance and all essential industry. The country liked many Labour ideas, but it did not quite trust the party to put them into practice without harmful effects. It was suspicious of interference with personal freedom. It saw that state control meant an army of government officials, with much waste of public money. After this first taste of Labour rule, the country put their Conservative rivals back into power for thirteen years before it let them try again. By then they had adopted more moderate ideas on government control.

The British people dislike extreme views, so that few Communists have won places in parliament ; but the name *fellow-traveller* is given to those who follow a Communist line. Since the war, Communists and their fellow-travellers have done much to disturb industrial peace and to weaken international confidence in British trade. They obtain influential positions in trade unions, where they stir up trouble and spoil the good work of honest union leaders. Their unofficial strikes cause great personal loss to the workers, as well as doing harm to the country.

Bad employers have been equally to blame. British industry was built up by the personal efforts of hard-working men. They formed companies in which the public bought shares. Too often the management then passed into the hands of unsuitable friends and relatives; but shareholders take even less interest in bad management than workers do in bad union leadership.

Though the problems of modern industrial relations are only slowly being solved, good wages and free social services have given the British worker a comfortable standard of living. His house may contain electric machines to wash clothes, to cook, to keep food cold, to heat the rooms. He can afford to wear good clothes, to drive a car, and to take his family for holidays abroad.

Such holiday travel has given him a closer personal interest in the affairs of other European countries, and this interest is reflected in the national press and in the schools. European languages— French, German, Spanish, Italian and Russian—are being more widely taught, not only in schools but in workers' evening classes.

Independence has loosened the ties of trade between the former colonies and Britain. This gives her the chance to play a fuller part in the commercial and industrial life of Europe. But her people are anxious not to weaken their friendship with the old dominions of Canada, Australia and New Zealand, which still attract many new British settlers every year.

In the meanwhile, Britain's children are growing up with a new outlook. To them, the empire is past history. They want Britain to be strong and respected, but they have no wish to be a World Power or to be responsible for keeping the peace in far-off places. Their international consciousness is expressed in support of world-wide causes like 'Save the Children', but their direct interests remain nearer home. Their future lies in closer union with the rest of Western Europe, where the English language is already valued as a basis of commercial and political understanding between the nations of the world. In the common search for peaceful progress, they have much to offer and much to learn.

Index

A number in bold type shows that the subject also appears on the following page or pages.
This index only includes the most important names and subjects mentioned in the book. Where subjects appear very often, such as Catholic or Protestant, only the most important references are given.